IT'S JUST A STORY
WE ARE ALL THE SUN
SWEET SURRENDER

Sunny Jetsun

'Sahaja' Inspired by Ananda Coomaraswamy 'The dance of Shiva'
'Wu wei', Creel, 'What is Taoism?'   * From Wikipedia *

It's Just a Story ~ We Are All The Sun ~ Sweet Surrender

Sunny Jetsun

Books by the Same Author:

Driving My Scooter through the Asteroid Field
Coming Down Over Venus ~ "Hallo Baba"
'Light love * Angels from Heaven
New Generation, Inspiration, Revolution, Revelation
All the Colours of Cosmic Rainbows'
'Green Eve * Don't lose the Light Vortex *
My brain's gone on holiday ~ free flowing feelings'
'Surfing or Suffering ~ together * Sense Consciousness
fields of a body with streams and stars of hearts'
"When You're happy you got wings on your back ~
Reposez vos oreilles à Goa; We're only one kiss away"
'Psychic Psychedelic'
'Streaming Lemon Topaz Sunbeams'
'Invasion of Beauty *FLASH* The Love Mudras'
'Patchouli Showers ~ Tantric Temples'
Anthology #1 ~ 'Enjoy The Revolution'
Anthology # 2 ~ 'Love & Freedom ~ Welcome'
'He Lives In a Parallel Universe'
'Queen of Space ~ King of Flower Power ~ dripping Rainbows'
'All Love Frequency ~ In Zero Space'
*Peace Goddess*Spirit of the Field*The Intimacy Sutras*
'Heavenly Bodies ~ Celestial Alignments
Feeling ~ Energy that Is LOVE in Itself'
'I've been to Venus & back*These Are Real Feelings*
Let the Universe Guide Your Heart*through Space'
The Kiss in Slaughterhouse 6

'Anatta * Anicca'

Mind*Body*Spirit ~ dhamma Consciousness of dukkha.
The root, spleen, solar plexus, Heart, throat, third eye,
crown Chakra ~ Samadhi Concentration of life's flow
Awareness is feeling mind*body infinitely changing
Observing omnipresent Sensations * equanimously

*

Antibodies

Drop the curse, stress, nerves, delusional pain, disorders.
Mass manipulator – no need to stand on your virtual head
or batter a defenseless pensioner, to eat their daily bread!
A Belligerent system, toxins in the body, digesting shame.
Throw it up to the wind, don't blame me.

*

Proton Pill Box

The Grim Reaper's rat a tat tat, horrible Death & Destruction!
Terrorised beyond your Imagination or dancing in Exstasis ~
'With molecules of bliss ~ Something must Exist'
Radio Active rocks, X Rays, Uranium Alpha waves, Radium.
Found subatomic particles in all the Oceans of the World.
Why so much Empty Space existing?
Had a leap of energetic genius ~
Making hay with nymphs while the sun shines.
Came back, Creative flowing, Can't Stop…

*

More Powerful Leprechauns

Spaced Cadet, "I do class A drugs all night and drink water"
I knew one guy stuck in a ditch on Ketamine ~ couldn't get out!
Choosing to hide in a K hole, than wanting to make love to me.
One snort too many, what's the point, taking the moment away ~
Blanked yourself out of our flow ~ resisting sensual Ecstasy.
'Krusties' ~ drinking & Ketamine, the Special K crew ~
Setting a pit bull on fire!

Re*Connection

Yes yes yes yes yes yes yes yes yes yes yes eyes
Inspired, living with the forest all around us ~
Sparking a memory ~ deep Inside themselves
Gotta have a Genie in the house ~ She's Magic
Another heavenly Celestial body basking in Potential.
Is it for Real, all my dreams came true.
Pinch me!

*

Giants of India

"I'm a forever lover of the divine"
Chilling out with Shakti's tribe.
Tantra Apsaras ~ Better than angels!
Call one in your meditation ~
she'll appear in your Orbit.
You have to have a connection.

*

As old as Shiva

'Who's this Monster of the Planet?'
You lose your heart ~ find your Spirit.
Tyrant's Sword method ~ Time to convert!
They'll let you take the crumbs.
Royal elephants crushing heads!
Let it be ~ what's it supposed to be?
All bollocks to growling, on extinct list, Tigers!
Tell the Satellites to fuck off! Criminally Insane.
Very Cruel, killing people to get their pot of gold.
It's a jungle out there, Yeah they're evil Predators.
"King cobras are very territorial, they will attack you!"
He lost all his powers ~ Alchemists' ripple effects
Come to Experience the best you can ~
Celestial sailing on an Ocean of Karma
To be free to feel her ~

Guava Goddess
A good bhang lassi in Varanasi
Smoked so many carrots ~
Looked at the river and cried for 3 days!
Last new year in a Temple with an Astronomer from Palenque
Going to Iguazu on the full moon ~
stepping inside the waterfall at night.
Full of butterflies.

*

Poetry in Motion ~ (not everything has a meaning)
'It's the message that counts not the messenger, the Message'
'Love is the message ~ the Message is Unconditional LOVE'
*"I'll go down with my Bubbles" * Bubbling ~ Changing.*
Consciousness of the Planet ~You can't STOP IT.
Enjoy it while you can ~ being in this present.
*'Visvavasu' ~ Beneficent to all*light getting bright,*

*

*Neolithic * Chemistry*
"First question ~ Do you take Ketamine or not?" ~ Anti Social.
Like to know what drugs they take, which downers & Uppers!
Ritual tripping ~ "Bong it in a Bamboo!"
Making DMT. tea!
Eating a rock after breakfast ~ Now that wasn't so bad!
Good on a nice day, when you got the beach to yourself.
*Thoughtless Awareness * A Light In an Ocean of Light **
90% of stuff going around your Mind is repetitive bullshit
Thinking about what will happen ~ not accepting the now!
Attention - Being in the moment ~ is flowing Consciousness.
Don't need the Info on Possession ~ do you FEEL Connected?
Things you can't explain; ultimately Life explains itself to itself.
You can't understand it ~You can be because You Are It.
Keep making those Mimosa cup-cakes ~ my best advice.
Dancing through Chaos

<u>Japanese for Lotus</u>
It flowers and seeds at the same time ~ causing & effecting.
Instant generation ~ Procreation.
"Nam Myoho Renge Kyo"
'Shit Happens ~ then More Shit Happens'
"I don't mind paying for the water if the women are Free!"
I like the Unity ~ Lovely and lusciousssssssss
"first time I'm dancing barefoot in the mud!"

*

<u>'Time Enough for Dystopia'</u>
The Car Park gang paid him a visit!
Unlucky with chopsticks, found one in his cranium
after 20 years, lucky to be alive…. not his time!
'Marijuana Is Wholesome'
"More human than human is our motto"
Fresh mangoes and peaches at the Yukon Hotel.
Genetic Cloud, A I. Redesigning your Eyes, Brain, Intel-Mind!
Added a Voiceprint Identification with a touch of Lemongrass.
"You think I'm a Replicant don't you?"
"It's painful to live in FEAR isn't it?"
'Cures Not War'

*

<u>Transcending Pain ~ within</u>
Wild flow of energy ~ She's putting it out to the World ~ Free.
Grass ~ its own life, swaying in the wind, with everything else.
How about Total Acid, Yellow Malana or Strawberry Cream?
MDMA all night, a Ketamine hole in bed, I like LSD at sunrise!
Do you think Goa's still on that Magic Ideal, Psychedelic trip?
Coca Cola's won the right to Ganga water and goats love hash!
Where have the dolphins gone, sold Kali to the highest bidder!
"You can't rip off the farmer's land, seeds, Ayurvedic plants;
You can't decide freedom for me, can't impose it either!"
"How much can you take ~ before you see the light?"

Through Realisation
Mitochondrial DNA through the female propelling Sperm cells.
"Politicians should Jam together before any negotiating!"
Communication ~ "Let's have an Orgy"; "Buy or you die!"
Who's got the biggest sausage?
All sorts of drops...
2.20 pm you gotta be stoned in Goa!
"I am not a number I am Unique."
"there's not many who are Free"
'Snake Charmer ~ in Tiger Park'

*

*Astro * Therapy Celebrate Together*
"I wanna lover ~ who takes some time"
Always wanting to desire it ~
Planting the next Unit....
It's all about Fear too.
All living the bollocks.
Gotta love the Surreal!
Living It ~ Cosmic Time

*

'What Women Want' - Program
"A vibrating, large phallic symbol, does what it's told,
makes the housework perfectly, brings in the dosh!"
They've had Robots in Japan for a long time;
Needs a stair lift ~ everyone has needs.
He developed feelings for you ~
Wanted to be classed as a Human.
Here is the Mystery of the Mind element.
"I Love Beautiful Women" ~ 'Intimacy without Intracrazy'
Erotic Sari dancers ~ immersed in C E L E B R A T I O N
"You can have everything I possess except Parvati"
Looking for the missing link ~ that doesn't exist!
All the freaks in the World ~ "I'm Welcome here"

Ginger
Gorilla in Love on a drum kit!
The missing 4%.
In love with an Orangutan
holding hands ~
*

Plasma Farms
Handing out Factory biscuits, Processed Pills as seen on TV!
Try photo voltaic LEDs; Gaia sending us Atomic Energy;
Bird's Custard, Apple Crumble, Frangipani essential oil!
Colours of Monsoon rainbows ~ Over the Irrawaddy.
We need rivers ~ torrents washing his house away!
*Raindrop season * Orchid blooms, sweet perfumes.*
*

The Key
Don't Worry ~ Be happy
That's a nice box you got there.
Went berserk with a wet crack ~ on the roof!
I met her ~ And got my belief ~ In Astrology.
Thought I lost a Terre byte.....
Last night, don't know what I said.
Not driven by a need ~Just Surrender
havin' Fun, maybe she likes Fun too!
*

Shrouded Barakah
"Tell me you love me"
"I don't know why they want to hear that"
"Why do women want to hear you say You love them?"
"I know Baba, because they wanna own you."
Female slaves in cloaks! Veils of separation...
Are they very open to brainwashing?
Alternative, Free energy ~ Pain relief.
Now Illegal to feed homeless people!

Desired Nothingness
Energy Abundance ~ Without the enormous Debt Tag!
Left us with a Paralysing Profit structure – enter Fascism.
'Integrity no Conditionality'
What's your Cause & Reaction?
We Are Everything complex ~ We Are Connected*Connectivity.
Don't Need any WMD. Nuclear, Military, Industrial Economy!
A Unified System ~ Natural holistic Symbiotic Synchronicity.
We Are All One ~ Unconditional LOVE
*

Fragmentation ~ Narrative
Religion put Faith to Control New Ideas, Vero Sig. Galileo?
Holy Belief is subject to Interpretation; 'Division of Palestine!'
Who was here first and whose God chose the rightful heirs?
MINE! It's time to change with what we know to be true today.
Let the Planet Live ~ let's develop in tune with Mother Nature
Not these Crazy, destructive, imperialistic, Fascistic Capitalists.
Insight into All the Systems NOT negative Hedge Fund betting!
Why STOP people thinking, subjecting them to Conditioned Identity?
*

Infinity Direction
Swimming around in different dimensions ~ Masters of Universe
Peace warrior eyeing a Jedi, nailed to a Cross and forgiving 'em.
You can go in forever ~ You can go out forever.
The Federal Reserve in Reality Guarantees, Perpetual DEBT!
Corporations carry out Government Policy on their own behalf.
'The moment you punch a time clock you enter a Dictatorship'
Use your Energy to transcend this State of Affairs.
*

SCREAMING
"Give me Drugs!!!!"
She had it there and then....

Lava Baba met Laser Baba at a Storm Rave
Hug Drug ~ Sensory perceptions tuned Up.
The failure of 'Just Say No' to Propaganda!
F E E L I N G ~ Serotonin, Consciousness.
'dancing in a sea of ecstasy'.
"Fascists don't want to change"
Government Exaggerating the Risks in Paradise ~
they don't know the Truth only their own Paranoia!
Officially lying about everything to destroy Public Trust.
"If you Smoke it you'll become a Heroin Addict!" Fake Media.
Budgeting for a Federal Bureau of Narcotics on the rampage!
Dropped out, Stoned and who cares about an horrendous War?
'Controlled Substances Act' the reason for more Police Dragnets.
"If you smoke dope bad things will happen but we don't know..
what they are." Trying shotguns in the DMZ. that you put us in!
People who wish to experiment should Not be Institutionalised
when not encroaching or hurting others ~ try that in your DMZ!
Who owns my right to Life, Liberty, the Pursuance of Happiness?
THC. CBD exposure; Cannabis the most popular drug in the World!
From UN. 1/25 people across the Globe use it! So what's wrong?
Three million people Criminalised under Clinton for inhaling weed.
1980/98, $214 billion for the War on Marijuana. Our Propaganda;
It's Nicer than Nice

*

You go for the Vibe
Goa Therapy, Local History! ~ Another reason to come back
because you feel at home, Shanti; "I finally found You here!"
Wanted a donation to a local Bio/Eco friendly village Temple!
He said "the Ganges was an Open sewer cleaned by the tides"
Visa Form - 'You can't Smoke Cigarettes and Kill Yourself but
you can dump Plastic & other bits all day and Kill the Planet!'
Living in the Collective brain ~ It's a Global Conglomeration!

Triggering*Cannabinoids

Dopamine Receptors ~ neurotransmitter filters
Craving ~ Psychological addiction!
Symptoms of physical withdrawal.
Drug free ~ No THC. on board.
We're all meditating together ~
told him to Jump ~ Psyche actively.
Exploring the evolution of Consciousness.
'While the Royal family owned all the Smack!
The CIA. Controls the Cocaine.' By Appointment!

*

Disenchanted Fillers

That was a good Mystery, Soul brother, Primal sister.
Energy of merging Consciousness ~ Inter Connectivity.
Electric field of Heart ~ has its own Cosmic Intelligence
Playground inside our pulsing skulls.
Telepathy in the Temple of the Spirit.

*

Integritydelic Guest

Preparation ~ Experience ~ Processing
¼ of animal species extinct in 30 years!!!
Our Expression of nature ~ Are you Awake!
We're Vibing together ~ gotta Keep Centred thru thick & thin!
Sanctioned torture ~ Global collapse of Civilisation!
(Mind) Only wants to Expand ~
Craving & being their hero - igniting phosphor bombs!!
Left my body hanging in a tree with Eros
Ecstatic state of luminous Consciousness.
Transcending on the good ship Lolly Pop.
Let's have a Magic dance ~
Astral traveler of the Psychelicious
Enjoy her ripe, fecund juiciness' irresistible Passion fruit.
Tuned to your subtleties ~ invisible code to my brain

<u>Gestapo State (Dispatches 25.10.2010 Channel 4)</u>
Northern Alliance sold Innocent men to the USA - cash bounty.
No tribunals, habeas corpus or basic human law for detainees.
'Psychological Interrogation Techniques' Not called, 'Torture!'
Sensory - 50 days Sleep deprivation, isolation; revive his heart!
CIA's 'Exotic techniques', Sexual Crimes, does dog tricks too!
Behavioral Science procreative, MK-Ultra spiked psychedelics.
Shackled Stress positions; Limited by your Imagination/sanity!
Developed 'Advanced Techniques' released a brain reaction ~
*

<u>Committed Together</u>
Your Loss ~ Thriving on Attention!
"I'm friendly but I'm not friendly!"
I like my Space ~
figure out if you want it otherwise get yu bus and go to Bombay!
"In the Tyrol you can drink the water from the toilet"
Gotta be on the same wavelength ~
"I Love you ~ You Love totally"
Feeling deep bliss bursting inside me ~
I want to go deeper ~ sharing it with you
*

<u>Sociopathic Master Races</u>
"When she arrives, have an American flag on the door!"
"God's fascist will sent us a tyrant like Hitler"
Digging their own graves and paid for the bullet!
An example to Slave populations! Imperial Model ~
Call to Courage to resist, could end in Ravensbruck,
a bullet in the back of her tortured, shrunken head. Bang!
WW.2.- 50 million people died, more civilians than military.
Explain how on Earth is this Madness allowed to happen?
Obedience to Perpetual War, let's Allow Symbiotic Energy!
Links to the 'Salo Illuminati' and all the other Inhumans.
Has a model of Darth Vader on his desk

The Land of Sensual Pleasure ~ 'Nave Nave Fenua'

'Flesh is Flesh * Spirit is Spirit'
Bird of Paradise subduing the Lizard.
Musical composition ~ 'Extinction of any horizon mirage!'
Sa chat noir ~ for extra spice, Sensuality ~ Meditation.
Chrome yellow pareus ~ In the presence of soft purring.
He's becoming a Maori ~ 'Prostitution is a Sacred act'
'Smallest amount of money can buy the mortal flesh'
Crushing the fruit on her body and giving it to me ~
Naked Super Humans climbing a gigantic coconut tree.
"You are lying!"
The fish have spoken; Superstitious divinity.
'By goodness evil is conquered'
Dream of the Painter
Mysterious waters

*

Play Station Generation

All In Cosmic Order ~ Psychedelic * Subliminal Zen....
Dimensional shifting ~ being Closest to her magnetic Moon.
Floating over the milky sea ~ serving his devoted Gopis.
Never felt so much in Control of Hot women in my life!
Knowing the circuits Inside out ~ Intense Reflexions.
Relaxing in the House of Orgasm ~ Primitive Desire.
The Passion of growth ~ becoming a Noble Savage.
Marquesan Red haired temptresses singing & dancing.
Why worry the sun rises every day? Re*birthing ~
Peaceful Spirit ~ sitting in silence by the Ocean
Addiction ~ carrying his ampoules de Morphine.
Escapism ~ Whose had a syphilitic heart attack then?
Exquisite fragrant Noa Noa parfum ~ on a languid breeze.
Living the complete life as a sweet native.
He moved into the jungle ~
"I am one with nature"

Red lithium*Yellow Sodium ~ Big Dipper
What's Opium used for ~ on the Astral Plane?
Is it the reason to go to War as we did before?
What are the addresses of the Chemical Corporation Tyrants?
Remote Controller ~
"Up to our neck in Terrorism!"
'Normal' ~ "How the fuck did I end up in this?"
Wearing the T Shirt, 'Psychological Warfare ~ A Police State'.
Spiritual/Conscious Liberation
*

The Love Factory
Spiritual hot spots, underground culture, bohemian dreamland
"Reaching Heaven however (we) define it"
Pictures from the Holy Mount Kailash ~ Resort.
I Like it ~ Religious Views ~ Forever ONE
*

'On the Speeding Gravy Train'
Pushing him to go ~ don't make yourself a Slave.
'It's my life' ~ 'Live & let live'
Met another muse with Nile green fingernails, violet eyes.
"Lost their conceptual piece on Hell" ~ flamenco foreplay.
'Challenging the way you look at things' try Ikebana!
Is there a Master Plan or is it all Intuitive flow?
"Bom Bhole" ~ Ask a Fauve
*

'Switching on Your Tree of Light'
'Love is all around' ~ Depends how close you are to yourself!
Something's going on, play of energies, synergies, let's see.
"What's she doin'? ~ gettin' stoned & gettin' laid!"
"You would Not say No"
"I chased her out the Ward!"
You gotta be Strong to Survive there.
Balance Problem

Free Field

Young Pikeys in free flow ~ Instinct!
Sticky Vicky with her Nightmare kit.
Without Ego you would have nothing left to let go ~
Missing the deep natural beauty ~ All the distractions.
Ego loves itself, "we hope so" ~ Let the snakes come out!
You never know if they got a gun stashed in the cupboard.
Going back to the full natural ~ not feeling sorry for yourself.
Zen Master waiting for boiled eggs on toast in the Gaia net ~
Human mind evolving where?
The Andean ones make you fly

*

Om vibrating the World

Let the music do the talkin' ~ "All I could see were Stars"
"I shall be spanking it this year Babe" In Candy Ville!
"Hey Baba are you a bit more coherent now?"
You don't need to have a memory ~ when you're here.
'This Is It'

*

"Just do it"

Connected to bliss ~ perfect on the beach.
The Earth is turning continuously and so are we.
You are experiencing it don't need the books or labels.
In bed with a baby snake, what to do? You play with it.
They Hijacked the Swastika, try some Swiss Reiki ~
Maybe they also Hijacked our Attention span!
To create that social identity waiting forever for their Messiah,
nothing to do with the current moment! Dive in now to heal it.
Where did you get your Paranoia? From the Best Exhibitionist!
All around shouting at us, "WAKE UP" ~ Living the colour.
Frequency of a flower ~ there's a floral shamanist out there!
Heard beautiful music, bluebells and daffodils vibrating.
Another kind of sound at different levels of Perception ~

Black Magic Gunther Uenker in a White Field. 1964
Welcome to wavy Bridget Riley and Dieter Roth ~
Don't support the corrupt, Global Conglomerate System.
They're never going to give up the MONEY, It's their God,
their Faith, their sense of Self-Preservation; no Democracy!
Obsolete thinking in a Pyramid, scheming, feeding their Idol.
Projected by a Oligarchic, faked Multi-Media.
Let's have some Abundance for a change ~
no need to be a Slave, Master. Eradicate Poverty!
"Always human behaviour not human Instinct"
Playing the magic in my head.

*

All Along the Dick Cheney Pipeline!
Went to War ~ 90% of Global production of Opium is for Heroin!
Ever heard of the Russell Trading Co; Corporate front of Raiders,
which is their Principal business? A Conglomerate revolution?
2017, 8 richest people have a greater wealth than the poorest
3 billion people; Sorry please repeat; 3 Billion fellow humans!
'Brown brothers & Harriman, largest Private Investment Bank
In the World!' Who are you giving your money to?

*

"It came from Up there!"
"Get 'em down your neck Baba!"
"Looking for a woman with the biggest age gap!"
Survival of the Ego, "can't blame a man for trying"
Does this thing work? Witnessing the Presence.
Eventually you stop thinking ~ Inner Clear Space
"Sometimes the Mind stops by Itself" ~ "tu es chez toi."
"For you to Surrender to that noise would be Incredible!"
Running it through a 'Cracking Program'
If you come from the heart, it doesn't matter.
How deep is Love? Stepping stones of Life ~

Venice ~ Wet Dream

"I was in Guatemala where I saw the best eyes and lips"
Tigers want to feel Love, "I love You" ~ Why not, simple!
Breathing Love ~ there can be no Secret about it!
Recycling funky inside ~ time is outside, being one.
House of the soul ~Transcending time & space.
Here's that Shit Life urchin, Ragamuffin
living in an Indian road labourers' slum!
Psychedelic surrealism ~ looking in the Psyche.
Inside the Mind, melting limited Mental-Forms.
Very trippy allegories.

*

Coke Can

Going pear shaped ~ 'A nasty pipe…
they can't take it up the nose or the arse!'
"There's strong and there's Strong!" Then there's Kali!
Crystal shickaboo…. A lot more Twisted on it!
Need more Father Christmases in Tehran.
"Let have a Crack pipe for Valentine's day!"
Bouncing Off…..
Metaphors of violations, Reflections, New Projections.
"Don't give a shit about the music ~ it's the dancing;
are you sure? Seeing who's on y/our wavelength ~
Anyone who can get the dance floor Rocking!"
Music makes you laugh, makes you smile in tune.
Got that funky beat ~ "I want to dance before I go"
Let's have a 4th dimensional Abstract ~ Gateway.
Dropping for Sunrise

*

Tundra Biome

Black diamonds ~ Cloudless Skies.
"Don't believe everything you read
Especially not this ~ "

<u>Apple's Crumbling try a Prana Yama Boccadillio</u>
A friend with very 'Special Needs' ~ Creative without destructive!
Found El Dorado ~ You go into eternity it becomes monotonous!
Going back to Zero, eating the Seeds looking at the manipulation.
It's in the Dettol. 1000% guarantees in India. Believe in it or not!
The Monetary system is Controlling Governments, Corporations.
Rockefeller controls 20 of the biggest Pharmaceutical Companies!
The Twin Towers in their Crosshairs + **M**utually **A**ssured **D**estruction!
Who owns the Money? Who makes the money? Where's it all gone?
Recycling Aluminium byproducts into fluoride, sensitive toothpaste!
Conspiracy of 'gotta get money at All costs' Lying thru their Teeth.
People need to see the crazy absurdity, to accept the truth
of giving up ~ nothing really holds on anymore!
They'll stop believing in the Institutions; sat by Pushkar's lake.
85% of people don't want to hear the truth ~ it's too Terrifying!
Pandas eating bamboo shoots, why not try a Uranium Spa?
Dropping E bombs over Jerusalem ~Totally Pirate shop!

*

<u>Chic to Chic</u> ~ Heaven or Hell, it's up to your Allowance...
Plastic Fantastic * I took the red pill went down the rabbit hole.
"Stop the Party ~ Captain Methry's run out of Class A drugs!"
Tantric makes you higher ~ being able in yourself to feel it.
Raw Chocolate Neurotransmitters supplying the whole brain ~
Essence of Space, being in that consciously, has its special tuning.
Tamed it down ~ 'doing the wrong things for the right reasons'.
"Don't like the sin but love the sinner" ~ for how long is Eternity?
Gave him Scrumpy-Jack in his pram; being a slave to a cigarette!
Try making some bhang ghee, charas butter from the mountains.
¼ on a bun would take you to the Moon, brings on Lunar whities.
They want to Control our reactions.
What do we do?
Integrate yourself into the big picture, wanting to see themselves.
"Do you know the price of onions has gone through the roof?"

Pleasure Giving

Finding the source of Narmada ~ filling with sunset crystals.
Living room with a special lingham, super Phallic energy ~
Entered the Paradise of Shiva. 'Life's on a nice tune now'

*

Feeling Super Heat

Brazil, You could smell the Kundalini!
Unfolding fragrant musical flowers ~
Loops ~ the beautiful harmony in Chaos.
It's just a Mind-concept you give yourself.
She understood, she is playing this attention game.
At the Temple of the Butterfly's Adoration.
"Nothing can harm you, it's all there for you"
Going to the edge and living it somehow....
Individual & multi*dimensional heart frequencies ~
You smell also what you live, we had strong smells last night!
"That's fake Cod fish"

*

Swami's Angels

The closest you can get to the light
Rhythms of the Universe ~
Sitting on a volcano of ecstasy.
"It's not Big busty but super tasty"
You want 'Availability' ~ all of my Presence.
"Emptied the joint bank account and went to Thailand"

*

Nurse Pam

"Go out of the church and get drunk" ~ From Mass to the Pub!
Decisions made by elders - Ensuring their Public respectability.
No words for 'Democracy' in their Primitive vocabulary! Why?
Cleaning out Opium pipes ~ filtration, processing for Heroin.
Got a billion Chinese to chase the Dragon!
'Crazier the better'

<u>Overdosing Time</u>
Inside don't know what Time it is ~ Cosmic spatial energy.
C O N S C I O U S N E S S ~
"Nobody knows how old I am"
"Why talk about Buddha, why not talking about themselves?"
STAY IN THE PRESENCE ~ don't want anything else.
*

<u>Planète * Beauté</u>
The Fear of it from your Mind will make you more sick!
A Powerful inner substance that speaks for itself ~
Very soft people trying to get into existence somewhere.
"Talkin' about arranging a Barbie evening….
"It stinks of Rock & Roll"
*

<u>Famous Black Metal Alien</u>
He's emphatic ~ "Everybody lies on Coke"
"I wouldn't mind meeting a sexy empath"
Females purring, feeling blissful
enough isn't it?
*

<u>Whacked Universe</u>
Bugs everywhere man this was the Brothel of the Black Mamba.
If you're gonna have a fuck have a full on Enlightening Fuck!
Just have to train those lips to move like velvet ~
"I don't want Heroin as a Christmas present thanks!"
That's a Big needle Baba! "My stamp came off in the sweat"
Birthday present, "A girl on my lap and I'm sucking her tits!"
Arriving in pseudo Paradise with such a wild Ketamine whore.
No talking in Trance, feel the energy ~ All different * One.
Look at that, the Sun rising between her legs.
You know a few Magenta fire dancers ~
"I'm Limpet Free" ~ Psycho bitch!
Everybody's got a Story

Quetzal Serendipity
The Mind is taken over the Computer's Calculations ~
Doesn't mean we can't use our Minds. Try super clarity.
"This jungle brew smells like Ayuhuasca when you cook it ~"
"Sue them so you can get another nose procedure for Free!"
'Moslem by circumstance' ~ we are the Rebels of Religion.
Living natural energy in an Amazon tribe, lost in synergy.
Washing the feet of a Goddess ~ sitting on a Volcano!
You're Reflecting her, don't go more in the hustle.
Let it happen by itself ~ whatever's happening…
Would you like to try, to fly?
The only way to know ~
*

The Big Crystal Scanner
Tuning into the sound of Sacred Geometry ~
No Fear anymore! Decoding Ciphers of Gematria.
"For sure Freedom is the best" * Consciousness.
You have to live with it ~ throw your Merkaba.
Gazing at the whole rainbow spectrum.
Children are it ~ we get it from them!
*

Psychedelic Myth
Not a meeting of conceptual minds ~ how can you own the Sky?
'When you process it you lose something of the Combination'
Is it true? 'The West lives in the future & East lives in the past,
Brazil & Africa in the moment ~ time doesn't mean anything.
'You can't Fix it' ~ Always in a flow Miss Romantic Herbalist.
"I want to cross the Ocean of Love with You"
Try a bio-Cosmic massage, detoxing a frayed nervous system,
regenerates your energy*feedback ~ It's Your Chi on holiday.
'Watching birds of Paradise ~ takes you to another World'
River Ghats-going down to the Source of Shiva lingams!
Crystalline swirls ~ sparkling along Omkareshwar's shore

'See you on the flip side'
What's Meditation about? Sitting & waiting.
Now I don't have to sit & wait ~ LIVING IT.
My firing little flame ~ in the heat of desire.
'Playing it from out of his heart'
If you can bring it over the feeling....
Dangerous stuff Sorceress' potions, melting me!
Why are you so Fearful? It's happening now ~
Animated circles dancing in the summer wheat.
Having a love affair with an Atlantean river Queen.
"In between ~ close your eyes"
*

Is it up & down or is it round & around
*In & out of spiral lingam Vortices * I'm sharing my Goa flow ~*
Streaming of dark matter's energy ~ molten Consciousness.
Treading their own path of pseudo Intellectual Propaganda.
Competitive, Judgment, Control, Identity, using Psychology.
You don't know what you think you know ~ It takes you....
Education ~True to Yourself,
Tribal vs Corporate Systemic.
If a reactionary to things who are you? How about these waves?
Spirit still dancing ~ losing yourself in the rhythm of Psytrance.
Jesus wasn't a dancer, or was he?
"I'd like to think he'd gone to a few raves"
Illegal, secret, fantastic, brilliant, wicked!
*

'Ishq' ~ Universal Love
"How come the Poorer the nation the bigger the heart?"
How far do you have to go to find someone on that Level?
Who wants to be the next Martyr for sociopathic wo/men?
Here's a non-delusional message from Scorpio girl!
"I Love this moment we're sharing together"
Enjoying no fear

Living Yoga

Tantra is letting go ~ being in the moment to moment
Plant the garden & let it grow ~ Higher & deeper
Smoke the weeds ~ Relax, Relax.
The Maharaja's favourite wife ~ Always Trouble.
Caused a family disturbance ~ Love is dangerous!
Consider blow up plastic dolls, least they don't bend your ear!
Be careful ~ We Love the laughter.
Very Juicy ~ get free popcorn.

*

A Triangular Screen

*Multi*Dimensionality * Flat Horizontal illusions ~ spiraling around*
falling off into Space ~ across curving, synergetic Ocean waves.
Take me as Indian not caste rated as a Moslem, Hindu, Sikh, Dalit!
Is that Norwegian Pan or Psychedelic Saint Germain?
Master of the violet flame, chohan of the seventh ray.
Spiritual Alchemist, expanding the blues ~

*

Trust to Trust

On a train to Varanasi with a bag of Mandy, bottle of poppers
& a nymphomaniac who'll never leave you ~ "Fancy a Fuck?"
You can be HIGH on Life can't you? Don't need stimulants!
We're so Full of Control/Programs! ~ How to get rid of it?
Jimi Hendrix with Electricity ~ Playfulness in the maze.
"Can I hold your hand, will you hold my hand?"
Changing in and out of the now ~ exploring.
Changing the Mind ~ Being in Acceptance.
"Do you want to marry me?"
"Then I saw how manipulating she was"
"Please help me I'm lost in a delusional, sociopathic haze!"
Have to be Together ~ on the Point or we're Separate…
Have to be Living in the Allowance State for it to happen.
"I should not forget it, I will be there ~"

Bondage Programs

Craving Attention ~ What could possibly go wrong?
"I Love tying them up, putting a knot in all the loose ends ~
Revelation in us ~ Full Consciousness. Tune in, communicate,
surrender, transmute. Don't/can't compare, all different; ONE.
Being the Perfect one to put all the fields in Order. Oh Yeah!
Which words to use when the Divine moves in you somewhere?
A Spiritual Revolution > the Mind naturally functions for survival
of its Ego; Spirit progresses in non-material, energetic Space ~
Scientific Observation * Dualistic Mind, splitting ~ Yin * Yanging
Tell the Mind "to do it!" Break all those deepest Attachments!
Intention to be Free ~ Eagles soaring in the sky above gravity.
Go for the Source*Always drinking from a clear, natural spring.
Pure living water it's all Perfect ~ Renewing the energetic Mind.
Computer on default ~ Automatic for the survival of the flesh, Id,
senses; let's convert it to Spirit ~ Life, & you're not a fat bastard!
Out of Mind, out of depression when you're forever dead; RIP.
This moment it is what it is Now ~ different things happening.
No future, learning to sow is there any need to Know or grow?
No tricky distortional brain taking you away with distractions,
doesn't want to give up 'Illusion' which feeds its own Identity,
evolution & destiny ~ Out of thought; No Time ~ Realisation.
Happy living life ~ in the lap of a responsive, fertility Goddess.

*

Singing Cockroaches

Frenzy ~ Feeding the Fear ~ it's all in the dream.
Tried some hash sausages, hot charas dogs. Acid Pie.
Chang & Tosh bangers; 'Beware Predators On Board'
Lovely Burritos, gotta stop doin' the MDMA! Woo, Woo!
Losing my appetite ~ 'Powers of the Mind to beguile'
Think of something, your Mind wanders to that ~
If in Love you're in Love ~
We create our own reality

Tantric Secret Weapons
Unleashed from denial!
Sitting next to supra-natural Shakti in a micro thong,
moaning, in the Perfect Place, at the Here & Now ~
She's a Yoga practitioner ~ going to energise the system.
You're going to experience who you are ~ what you are not!
Free TV's ~ 'Thanks for letting us into your living room!'
Designed to maintain a sense of paranoia and fear.
Treadmill building blocks for Social, mass Control ~
Bring the Press show them how good it can be.
Alpha animals on the loose ~

*

Came to be a Coconut Personality
It wasn't reverie ~ dropped off the Palm tree ~
into a barrage of constant negative Potentiality.
Make Peace with it, explain it direct & clearly.
"What we're looking for on the Outside is a mirror ~
reflection of our integrated fe/male on the Inside filigree"
Making this Tantra connection ~ retained in you.
Raising up the model of Perfection

*

It Never Comes
"I'd go mad if they ate my Candyman"
Anything that moves they'll put on a plate!
Where's the Value being added to the System?
'Imaginary ~ tomorrow everything is for FREE!'
Saying **Yes** to everything, why not?
Not surrendering yourself to any Fear.
Running after the Signposts, just want the experience now.
"If you forget everything * you remember everything"
The hot rush from a naked beauty swimming in an Infinity pool.
Goa Attraction ~ distraction after distraction after distraction.
This is Heaven not Hollywood

Witness In Complex City

Feel like you already have it ~ because it's already there.
We're not here to resist ~ & those who come in FEAR
Instead of feeling the Fear, do it anyway! don't stand still!
'More or Nothing' ~ "to get is animal, to give is human" Ideal.
The Focus is always on getting More ~ money, material people.
A need for something to blame ~ No Growth ~ Nothing Inside.
Based on this stress to be in the right position,
means you are higher ~ Looking down from Up.
I Stop this bullshit ~ let's keep to the moment.
Listening to the past ~ a safe way of keeping away from now.
In that sense the future's already ~ free and easy
This wave of Freedom carries you over ~

*

Psychedelic Hacienda

Mental Torture that's the Best!
Extraordinarily emotional is pretty good too!
A Big blocking Constipation ~ resistance against flow
Everything came after that ~ New Order. Still being in Trance.
Sometimes believing is all it takes, wanna be happy, Start now.
"All she's gotta do is just turn up" ~ without Energetic diarrhea.
I've done all my Yoga, beam me a light!

*

Tantra Lesson Caves

A plate of special cup cakes went missing.
The first solar, bio*energetic Heart Bypass ~
3 guys in a room peddlin' - keepin' you goin'
Live It ~ Be It, I'm not Thinking! 'Under dosed...
Not taking enough * full pharmaceutical Motherboard!
Very basic ~ Singing deep in Mother Earth
It bangs on Immediately ~ Shine and Smile.
It helps you smile ~ if you got something to smile about!
Perfumed Yoni, pouring fresh double cream

'If you have a Yoni Honk!'
Bitch, "I've got FEELINGS too!"
Super Emotional ~ Different expectations, needs, wants!
She really loves you, you'd better listen ~ Stick lips on 'em.
"Do you love me darling?" ~ "Yeah I'd love to fuck you"
Roxanne feeding me sweet mangoes, sucking me down deep.
Class A whore ~ with a right hook, a nutter nutted me nuts,
could have been sectioned instead of Shanti on the beach.
Going from Hell to Ecstasy!
Took me into the Madness, playing with a gorgeous Gopi.
"Look I moved on ~ be happy"
*

Psychedelic Continent
Trance has nearly finished, more chill out than Raves.
Poker ~ "Instead of playing cards I was playing my ego"
LSD narrative ~ the lesson is everywhere as it should be.
Dumping ground, ex boy/girlfriends on every street corner.
The future can't be better than now ~
'No Place like the Goa Syndrome'
*

Tandava Delight
Magic Carpet ~ "Fuckin' hell Baba get a Grip!"
Fondling an Avatar of Sex, exploding Chakras!
"There's a good Indian woman under all that violence!"
Can't make her step into that fire anymore with a cheering crowd!
"They want to make a bubble around us." Dancing of Destruction.
Kali's Temple, the Ghats, Varanasi buying hash from a street gang!
Calming Hallucination, facing our own deepest fears from Inside out.
Lots of Specialists here, entering a fire area ~ A Theatre full of War!
Armed to their teeth; all the previous knowledge is worthless ~
The flow ~ Be it ~ it is just becoming now.
Sitting on the river ~ You are the river!
SPLASH

<u>Classified Magical</u>
Rapids ~ White horses galloping in the river.
"The Angel fish are swimming in your living room"
"Were you singing mantras with your soul in Phnom Penh?"
"I don't like being where they don't look after the Plastic story"
From herbs to Roots moving you into a different enzyme energy.
Blink of the eye ~ She's nice, dreaming, reading a book, gazing.
No fear at all, "but I'm scared, so never been back to the past."
They have loads of Scrap, in Scotland, a few Palm trees too!
"I love to lick the pot!"
Thrown on the fire ~ burning
Transmutation of the material.
Full Shiva * Shakti Power
*

<u>Capt. Planet</u>
Transmuting densities through Your Mind filled with Love ~
Resonating over the Heart, becoming dimensions of Wisdom.
Sexual Frequency ~ It's beautiful that you had that exchange.
Personal to the Trance Planets ~ She's Uranic!
Ultimately the Attachment, locking us in gravity.
"No more a Place, it's beyond States of Mind"
Spent his life in DMT * Outer Cosmic Space
Ascended Masters are with You for the Best.
To Open up for Inner Spirit ~
*

<u>Do or Die!</u>
START ~ Unconditionally Loving.
"Love yourself first mate." Transmit,
if you got no love ~ can't share it out.
Gotta Love <u>Inside</u> Yourself * Yes You!
Compassion for others ~ generating the Overflow.
"All You Need Is Love"
Sparkling!

Found You - She went to Crack City
It's as real as you believe it to be real ~Tuning into You beauty.
Welcome to Life, how do you say, 'Thank you' in your language?
The Innocent Child stuff, you believe anything when you're a child!
Feel like you already have it ~ because it's already there.
If everyone's tripping you trip, entering their Consciousness ~
It's Ego, people think they know everything, the chillum's trippy!
Chakras doing figure of 8's then you went to her Paradise Space
where Consciousness can be altered
*
Martian Probes
Vibrations flowing UP ~ full on Visual Psychedelics.
Om vibrating the World, Inside of You Cosmic Kitten.
Regenerating itself, we're Atomic Bombshells going off!
He needs more than Retail therapy ~ a light sleeper awake.
Your Focus is your energy ~ Your Mind, telling You; Feel It!
Ultimately You don't have to think about it to Understand it ~
feeling a pure gentle breeze
*
Viscosity
"Buddha didn't want any Buddhism" ~ Why not liberate us all?
Energetics breaking the old karma & making new Presumptions!
Don't know where the day went! Who knows where any day goes?
Dying for the lights, colouring puncture, now I'll work on your heart.
"Strap a plank to me arse in case I fall in." "Are you sure Baba?"
"Nearer the bone, the sweeter the meat" Opening Star attraction.
"Everyone's got the potential to be artistic same as to be autistic"
Emerald Planet of natural serenity ~ tuning into the orbiting Sun.
*Allowing that higher frequency to take over * Altruistic....*
Piercing her mushy, is it wrong or what? Sweet laughter.
Tao movements ~ hugging a tree for Nature's Life Force!
Love being off my head by the Ocean of an Open heart ~
surrounded by the bliss Babas, Sat Chit Ananda

Enlightenment Is Changing
Ultimately ~ It's a continuous process, processing….
Understanding its motivation ~Time & Space flow ~
We will make new families out of the same wavelength ~
Unfolding Consciousness
My thought processes creating ~ creating My disillusionment,
My suffering, My bliss; Free from being a Slave to My Mind!
Vomited Iridescent butterflies ~ I Love fractals, Visuals.
Why do I have a sense to move into the future ~
Allowing it to be

*

Officially An Om in us (Ask wikipedia for any Info.)
Island of Screams ~ "I'll never go back" Full Blood lust!
and we were starving, being wrapped up as mummy ~
chased by a gang of maniacal children with empty, lost eyes.
It enlightened, freed my Mind from limited Mental-Formations.
"Let's have some Sacred Nuclear War!" Guess who said that?
Independent Journalists' Cameras 'mistaken' for weapons ~
Sitting in an Apache, following the 'Rules of Engagement!
Shot them all to bits including the two babies!
"We regret any loss of Innocent civilian Life"

*

Extraordinary Pros & Cons
State Sponsored Terrorism! Government deceit/Disclaimers!
On the Edge of Anarchy ~ going to the next Level (of Insanity).
Redux ,1984 Revisited - Preemptive Murderers, body searches!
Intergalactic Landscape ~ Here & not there, All Bombed out!
"They want to have a Fucking Sacred Nuclear War!"
Attached to the concept of Me & thee; apostasy!
It Enlightened my Mind! Dropped the Infidelity!
Absolute Power's Abuse ~ Obsessed, Oppressed!
Last defence of the Realm, Reptiles in the Palace!
"Let's All Live PURE SUNSHINE Consciousness"

28

And we're in the Kiss!
"He got cancer and all he wanted to do was eat a chicken.
His last wish after a Macrobiotic life ~ then he has died!"
Inspiring ~ Giving Thanks ~ is Meditation in the moment.
Let's fall in it ~ Be Who You Are.
Allowing the kiss from the sky to mother Earth.
Falling in the flow ~ of celestial psytrance music.

*

Lolita Shakti, 19 & 38 kilos
Making circles ~ going Up.
Falling into a black hole ~
They took you to the Edge of the Vortex Baba!
Opening of the Gate ~ some kind of Ceremony.
'1ˢᵗ man up last man down'
"Did I come with a bag or not?"
It's not my thing ~
"I heard about your last Shamanic experience"
"First of all they should Unpollute their country!"
This sanitation is fucked up ~ Keep in touch.
"Didn't even feel her on the back of me bike"
A great inspiration ~ flirting Hippy butterfly.
She was singing her songs in Swedish.

*

This is the Magic
for it to come through the Space.
Give way ~ Yourself is in the way!
You can blow at once all her facets.
'Since he let go ~ now he knows what Freedom is'
You have to go through it & Know why you would let it go!
He's playing golf in Tripoli, no cares, as healthy as can be…
270 people are rotting in their graves at Lockerbie!
If you're on the Hot seat ~ you're on the Hot seat!
"Aye Caramba, a South American Senorita!"

Synchronicity: we can't say it anymore so you make new words...
Seeing all the connections into the Space ~You bring two
or three dimensions together and put it in one word;
Since your Lifetime ~ is one eternal moment

*

Black Eve

"I trust his face ~You see it"
Doesn't get lost in his thoughts.
Sita's singing the Bossa Nova.
"My Psychedelia's from birth
I brought it with me ~ "
'Existence Itself is Psychedelic'
"It's there otherwise it wouldn't be there"
"Take a nano-chip in your arm ~ for Future Planning!"
It gets more and more clear, that people don't Trust.
The less Trust the More Control ~ but I/we really lose.

*

'Stairway to Goa'

The Psychedelic, Bliss Babas ~ Going with the fluffy stuff.
India's full of Pickles ~ Sailing to Baga, riding to Chapora!
"You're old enough to have a bit of discipline ~
Obsessed by Nitrous girl. "You just like blacking out!"
"It's all in here ~ just have to see it"
Hills full of Magic mushrooms, you can buy Medical Clones!
Snorkeling on Acid * Super colorful, multi*dimensionality.
"I know I am his heart ~ I am what makes him happy"
"Take me to Psilocybin City"

*

Dolphin Insult

Endless Summer ~ bringing bliss, throwing Lotuses.
Watching the stupid madness unfolding in front of me!
Got her in the walking process ~ from the cucking stool.
Taking the wrapping off ~ "I was Happy once!"

30

'Azadah' ~ 'Freedom' in Farsi.
XXXXXcess*More & more greed in the heart ~ Send them Love.
Now to straighten out the guys who bent themselves for money.
That's when I knew the Hard core people!
'Time doesn't mean anything at the moment'
In that very instant ~ when the body broke apart.
Too many drugs, crashed out on the ground in epilepsy.
"The one who calls the ambulance, doctor; pays the bill!"
Going through the tumult…..

*

"You are already in heaven"
Bursting your Love light out ~ You're enflamed!
"The Venusians sent her to me ~ on Pleiadian Starship #69"
She's the Deluxe Love Model.

*

Mother of Pearl Avatar
Let's go to Thailand ~ and look for Shiva eyes.
More imprints coming up now ~ with the Metatron.
Slow down ~ they smell your embedded Fear!
The Process of being in doubt ~ to learn from it.
Reflections from the other side ~ two fields into One.
"Give them Shaktivari they can handle 100 husbands!"
Indian Asparagus root entwining in my Wild Winter Cherry.

*

Rainbows dela Poesia
Going out with the Intention ~ to be Open.
Triggering women's emotions, going straight to the Point
'You can't show someone something if they're not ready to see'
Giving it a Higher state ~ 'A kiss from the Sky'
Which is real Tantra
He got it from beautiful Rumi ~ I like Sufi free style.
Omar Khayam on a summer day, relaxing in the shade.
Caressing a little berry

Weird Consistency

Satanists recruiting **YOU** in their War on our Consciousnesses.
Multi dimensional Simulator ~ through Seamless virtual realities.
He has died so many times ~ feeling it to be natural as he's free.
You're over yeasting darling, living in tents can't afford cement.
Dancing barefoot in the sand as Shamanically as can be ~
Cosmic Currency ~ the river scenes are flowing timeless*ness.
Open minded touch, make a connection with the floating Orbs
they show themselves to some; sun rising inside crop circles.
"There's a lot of electronics coming out of this body!"
Took out the 82cms. Big Excalibur.

*

Cool Crew

"I think I'll have to Institutionalize myself to do Yoga"
'WAR ON CONSCIOUSNESS'
Let's play some 70's Cocaine music!

*

Angel Consciousness

"One wo|man's Freedom Fighter is another wo|man's Terrorist!"
Duality on the rest of US ~ Try an aligning Energetic Therapist!
Coming back from having a Transmission
"When I put the Star in the Heart
everyone is different ~

*

No Brainer

Tantric Films ~ Gotta get it on reel, getting into the dance!
"We can only enjoy the moment ~ there's nothing else"
Buy an Island near the Equator, in that chocolate Zone.
Eating it raw, everyone being happy ~ onto 'Next Levels'
What is a practical solution? Letting it happen all at once.
'If the product is good, the action is good and Vice versa'
Can you eat happiness? Happiness is already in your mouth
but you don't realise it

Chinese Secret Society

100,000 Ninja assassins en route, coming to City Palaces.
If you've been targeted by them, pray for a miracle Baron!
Who are they? We can't discern their vibration ~
They gave Rothschild, Rockefeller Co. a fuckin Adrenalin rush!
Living in a World of numbers, 1 for this, 4 for that, a million here,
1/5 there and the total destruction, 0 coming tomorrow or
is that 1 day after tomorrow to our 7+ billion inhabitants?
He has this much more to survive than his 10 starving children!
How do we break the light to see the point? Give them a Prism.
All Illusions & Conditioning, Mr&MrsMade&SpiedonIdentity.com
Down that line ~ tune it as it is, hologram realization.
Experiencing its Potential ~ duality, relativity & reality.

*

Coral ~ Flower of the Ocean

There's nothing more Funtastic than a Full Psychedelic reef.
"You can jump into my day Cherie"
Getting rid of all of her heart pain.
Binded her ~ to the moment, she was falling out.
There was a miracle yesterday!
The Synchronicity is Stronger.
HEALING * FEELING

*

Nice word 'Darshan'

Kali is the One who takes it in and digests it!
Eats up All the Negativities ~ from Mahamaya.
Underground Avatars * roots feeding the Earth.

*

Astrological Alignments

Tuning of the dwarf Pluto's minor Moon, different Vibrations ~ resonance.
"You have to meet someone who has achieved the State in his own
Consciousness ~ to manifest the gift and give it out to others"
Deeply for Mother Earth ~ Lets the energetic Chi flow strong.

Very trained brain

"I like my vices ~ I embrace them!"
A Police State - "It's back to the illegal raves then!"
"Since when has it been a crime to be a Suspect?"
"Fuck the World, it's comin' to an end anytime soon"
Short termism keeps us from wanting Revolution or even change.
To the Controllers Free thought is a Danger on the High street!
Keeping us fully cloned in hyper shopping malls, mini corporate cities,
sanitized parks, sponsored schools, themed housing communities.
Private Security forces, taking away all y/our rights at festivals
banging the shit out of you behind the wall!

*

Butterfly Whirlwind

Toxic body, LSD for migraine, "Does it work?"
"It takes your mind off it" Psychedelics of course ~
When she smiles it's Summertime; a Spanish ball of fire!
"If I am immortal why do I want to come back to the body?"
"I want a girl who'll do special Puja for me in the morning"
"Met her in the chai shop, this gipsy spent all night"
"You are Protected, No Active Threats" - I'm not in your gang!
"Gotta go she's licking the table,
Crystals everywhere ~

*

The Russian Explosion!

Gorgeous Roxannas, playmates on every beach.
"You look very beautiful in a sari" ~ live bliss bubbly.
"Take some more chemicals"*"I can't go back to reality now"
Feeling the Banyan tree's enormous wall of vibration ~
"What is the intention in Art, any kind of art?
Fully expressive, to come into the moment ~
We got Music under our arse ~ everywhere..
It's happening ~ it's now not even a process.
"Fresh water is coming from?" ~ "The sky!"

Will Power

'The Information Highway ~ in streams of Light'
Only going through desire ~
The right fly for the right trout……
'Everything is new under this Sun'
The Bliss Molecule*dissolving mountains of memories.
Neurotransmitters in raw Chocolate ~ the allowance to be.
Children living in each moment ~ electrochemical impulses.
Connecting the synapses in your brain ~ keeps your vitality.
What sort of signal do you want to resonate to the Universe?
'Already there ~ Not putting something there that isn't there'
Religion controls right hemisphere, emotions, ability to smile.
Dictating logic, Mind Movement and Control Consciousness.
Show me the Natural Highs

*

Acid Hologram

What a load of bollocks ~ And I wasn't listening either….
she's always looking for an answer to this & that & me & her.
Maybe there is no answer, maybe that is the answer, to what.
"Only dead fish swim with the flow ~ others swim against it!"
Two new moons shining through 5th dimensional windows.
Entering at the end of a fifty year cycle ~
Need a holographic code to Open it all up.
Crossing its Orbit weaving with everyone else!

*

Golden Sun with Wings

Sat chit Ananda, enhancing what's already in the cake!
'Aces from the Heart' ~ Organic try Permaculture vitality!
Learning the difference between 'Need and Want'
Corruption Kills! Better embracing the Love vibe ~
Some people don't know when they have enough!
"Darling take that bone out of your nose,
do you think you're in a primitive tribe?"

Open Party

My soul has passed through Atlantis ~ I am from Cosmic being.
"I was snorkeling in Honduras at Timothy Leary beach"
Nuclear Power is Ancient technology, try Plasma balls!
Spiders in the jet stream, flying through outer Space.
A Mayfly only lives for a day, a dragonfly a fortnight ~
Try some Aphrodisiac, Fertility Chocolate Vapours.
"Hustling in the name of Christ"
They don't want to teach you how to think.
"In my mind I got that naughty girl feeling."
Getting the contracts to rebuild the crater that was Baghdad!
Haliburton Corp. laughing all the way to their Cryptocratic bank!
When you Control the mass-media you can sweep all that away!
Creating a short term memory span.

*

Columbian Coke Car.

"I was in love with a lesbian yesterday"
The Space ~ No space; Everything!
'The Truth Is' * "The Best Christmas ever!"
Found a female python coiling around your hot sex charka.
Is it called Kundalini? "Got to go where it's possible ~"
"Do you know how many times I've been to the possible mate?
'Tweaking the girl in a sexy black lace Funder bra'

*

Kundalini Devis

"From New York - did she smoke crack?"
"No they're immune to any drugs"
'Magical 4th dimension where you can shift elements,
All falling apart ~ Mind is basically, constant 'duality'.
Or a tool of discernment, learning about polarities
Learning how to use your free will ~ Relativity.
"Let the demons come out and Celebrate!"
"Welcome to the Pain Club" ~ Then you let it go

<u>Maar's Collection</u>
Their Master pieces ~ "They're full of feeling, joy, full of life!"
Met her at 'Les Deux Magots' on Avenue Germain des Pres.
Asked her if she'd been to Lake Titicaca; She spoke Spanish,
full of the heat of inspiration ~ her fluent tongue of Surrealism.
A Member of the French Communist Party from the beginning.
Part of the movement.

*

<u>Venus' Love Virus</u>
I gotta lot in me ~ don't forget some Magenta, darling.
Esmeralda's green is the colour of her 'Sahasha' chakra.
"You come from a tradition of Romantic Poets & Poetesses"
Intergalactic landscapes ~ Rosy Spirit feeling in my Heart
Dancing with the divine ~ staying in the Abundance
'The treasure is Trust' "I want to be a shiny Star!"
Lighting it Up! The picture ~ Space Light.
'We are all the Sun'

*

<u>'Pure I fire'</u>
Choosing, "Why didn't someone see it this way before?"
From the front, from behind, not signed ~ Free to see.
Revelation of streaming light from within Pixie glades.
Incredible colours, textures, shapes, forms and shades.

*

<u>Surreal Birds at Hotel Amsterdam</u>
"I don't want to be surrounded by objects"
Came back ~ Can't Stop the creative flow
Juicy, tastiness, a perfect ring ~
Frame of Mind ~ The Intention Experiment.
"I'm a Green Man, very Kinesis Green!"
Energetic Crop Circles in a Zero point field.
He made his Magic, his wife drank blood ~
Listening to a Nagger Baba from west Bengal

Ignoble Authority
Violence Hard Wired ~ Let's have a law for Emotional Rights!
"The People on the top want to steer us right onto the Rocks!"
They love to make money, profiteering from Diabolical deaths.
They Need Crime waves to feed the Apparatus of their State!
Otherwise why are you paying Taxes for Protection, Security?
What are your results, latest Figures, trends that we asked for?
Ask the Head scientist of HMS. Government Committee on drugs
He resigned over his proven figures being thrown in the bin ~
by the Inquisitor

*

MOD
"36 mirrors on my bike
Big Flag on the back
A Target on the front ~"
I've had some Hawaiian mushrooms
Got lost in the jungle, on Brighton's pier!

*

Transient Star
His flat on fire! Lost it all and got Liberated!
Final nail in the coffin of Attachments ~
"What can you do it's all gone!"
None of it meant anything ~ just Stuff.
"But I love the view ~ & reality is still going on"
You get on with it ~ they want the wobble, learning the heart.
"Didn't see anything I was down at the beach"
Fully Insured ~ stood in the wreckage!

*

Gives it a nudge ~
drops...... a bubble on me!
If it makes you relaxed ~ it's healing.
Gone out of the body
Sit down and hold onto the Planet!

Living * ART
All sense of giving
It is like Heaven ~
Happiness on Earth
A Spiritual Temple
All these light workers
Connecting sunbeams everywhere.
Gateways ~ to the Angelic realm
*

Celestial Spectra
The Quality of Fear! Manifestation, from your deep insides!
The idea is to go out of your Mind ~ Being centred in Clarity.
How we Visually Perceive ~ Reality of our Galactic Hologram
as Consciousness ~ into energy fields * collapsing into matter.
We are mostly empty Space in a Cosmic, virtual spider web ~
Santa Fe veils are thin there; Everyone's living their own truth.
Who are you ~ to Judge? It's all y/our own, Interior Projection!
The Heart Aware ~ It's Alive
Try the Quantum Jump * feeling Mut's astral Reaction,
being subatomic ~ ripples throughout the Universe.
Brilliant Mirrors & Reflections ~ No words, thoughts.
Don't need any Pathological Obsessions with detail.
*

Agni & Indra
More Massive Fire Power! Daisy Cutters strimming!
"He's not just someone who throws out Cosmic Rays"
'Please come down for an evening of high jinx with Caligula'
"You keep throwing a spanner in me works!"
"She's not ultra paranoid".... "that's good"
"Language is a virus, we're all infected by it"
Who's Protecting the Balance of Life?
'Pre-Emptive Attack' Some Shock & Awe! Have some More!
"We'll fight Terror with Terror" ~ We'll get there before them!

Reign*Carnation
"Can't be any worse!"
Asking for a Miracle

*

60 beautiful Moons around Saturn
Shining in the Sunlight, Icebergs floating in the lagoon,
100's of bright ringlets, billions of separate particles ~
Yin*Yang sparkling infinite miles from Earth.
Titan bigger than the planet Mercury!
In the heart of her E Ring

*

Pachimama's Tiger Lilies
Lilium Superbum alive in an erotic landscape ~ free flowing
Irrawaddy, Bora Bora, Morea, Java, Sumatra, Annapurna ~
'Goddess of the harvest' ~ Mythological names, lovely poetry.
Design Revolution, Aung San Suu Kyi on top of the mountain.
The temptation of another love apple, he could see the sea ~
Paid poor working girls to talk to him - Enter: English, translate.
Spent some time in the Yellow house, Maison of Pleasures
with descendents of the Aztecs carrying Torches of Desire ~
It's Vibrational ~ Palenque, the Goddess Temple in pulsation.

*

Tesco Togo
Ate wonderful Blue Cheese, melted onto delicious Liberty caps.
Who needs genetic Proof, look into her lips and sparkling eyes.
Some say they were targeted by Reptilian hybrids in Budapest!
Who was interbreeding with your ancestors on that May day?
Memories of the Holy Byzantines ~ carried in their bloodlines.
Those who kill their brother, rape their sisters enslave the rest!
Did you find that Maya in the Kabbalah, Casbah or Jambalaya?
'Try a set of esoteric teachings meant to explain the relationship between
the eternal & mysterious creator, the mortal & finite universe (Creation)'.

The Worst of the Worst
Threw the Geneva Convention in the Executive rubbish bin.
Let's have more Water boarding ~ Strategy of their Satan!
Put him in a box and Rendered him for his own protection!
Telling you what he thinks the Interrogator wants to hear!
Revenge coming down Route 66, "Salam Alaikum" folks!
Brothers in Hi Vis Orange, dog collars & prison bracelets
on their way. Violations, a ticking bomb called Abu Gharaib.
War Crime Acts of a President and his Neocon Administrators.
Congress bows to Democratic Dictators of a dead constitution.
Living over fault lines ~

*

Mercury Messenger
"Your body is a vehicle for your Consciousness"
Orbital resonance, alignment, the angles are the same.
We're part of the Solar System.
Forces of gravity acting on the moons of Neptune.
What's smashed into a string of exploding Comets?
Neutrinos' heavy bombardment creating craters ~
What is the behaviour of sand in the Martian desert?
Dunes as far as the eye can see * 3.6 billion years of chaos!
What are the patterns in the F rings of Saturn?
Prometheus and Pandora turning inside out.

*

Tiger Stripes
Volcanoes, fountains, geysers, thermal hot spots, nebulae,
blasting plumes, exploding wonders of the solar system....
'Sky's the limit' reflects ice crystals on ET's crashed spaceship.
Conquerors have passed before and left a lot of blonde children.
Don't write that you'll have Jihad on your back, hurling abuse.
The arrival of the Papacy in his bulletproof car & Swiss guard.
Phalanx of orange fluor vested police, Security corps to order!
Holy Propaganda in the name of the Father, Son & Holy Ghost

Geomancy ~ dragon harmony
Horrified by dead pigs ~ what are you getting?
He wants to be a Goa Policeman in his next life!
"LSD is not the problem, it's about your Mind's Abuse"
Dancing with the molecules of infinity ~ Consciously.
Afraid to go in the doors of other realities ~ when
*You can't get more Multi * cultural than that!*
"Free spirit ~ don't want a religious experience"
Juicy juicy juicy juicy spectrum
*

Iridescent Tonic Suits
"What do I do Doctor, do I take another 100 mikes?"
Hooked on Craving ~ for the Smart sweeties.
'Plot to dope America' from whom?
"In Missouri 2 joints will get you life!"
Talk about Criminal Paranoia Syndrome, Gestapo trying this!
Another Extreme, Exaggerated Power of a (Holy) Inquisition!
Scare stories, fear in everything ~ Variations of 'Demoncrazy!'
Outlawing marijuana around the whole World Dictatorship.
And another Federal War on happy, Intoxicated, sleepy people.
Discovering altered consciousness.
To Rise above is Enlightenment
*

Crowned & Crucified
Shaven black ~ Pink inside, a lovely taste.
You can't see Paradise anymore ~
"don't be so heavy handed with my lips!"
Russian Panther at my local, Shiva Valley.
Baba need to change your filters.
Doing the night shift at Sellafield.
'Factory Happiness'
Being full ~ filled in the moment
IS LOVE

Roots & Ruts

2nd chakra lovers in Brazil * sipping Tantric Mohitos ~
MDMA Groove ~ Pure Hedonism, hearing the serenade.
Be Conscious ~ Don't do jealousy; Enjoy what you do.
Standing on the terraces, nearly disintegrated ~
Epicurean catalyst; who invented the word 'Psychedelic'?
"Paying them $40 a day to take LSD. as an experiment"
Leaking out of the Laboratory ~ Give them a Lobotomy!
Took from the hands of Shamans given to the Chaotic public!
Journeys into mythical Revelation; a generation on trippy Acid.
Riding the Prankster bus * Extra sensory * Superb fully immersed
In Infinity ~ Moving from Inside
*

A Craze

In the Insane Asylum, 'turn on tune in drop out'
Painted it bright colours and loaded with Acid.
A free experience ~ in Mind Expansion
Abusing Sandoz * LSD on the street!
Who wants Instant Liberation!
*

Vibrating Sweeties

"I can do Everything" Astro*Therapy, Great New colours.
Love the psychedelic, natural, hippie life of free spirit.
Creation ~ Unreal, drop out with a microdot!
Escaping the World * Whose Exaggeration?
Who's crossing into the dark side!
The fossils came Alive........
*

Suck it in and see!

Why they built Hadrian's wall?
Wild Heather, Scottish women!!!
Laws to exploit the Obedient masses.
Your own Colon cleaning for Free!

43

<u>Good for People!</u>
Resource based Economy
Not a Money based Society!
Elite basing the world on Scarcity & Slavery.
Harvesting the New Sun * Energy Availability.
Geothermal coursing in the veins of Pachimama
Using Technology properly, we are one species ~
She's a young Brazilian ~ beauty!
Symbiotic Unconditional Love

*

<u>Private Federal Reserve</u>
Modern Money Mechanics
'Fractional Reserve System'
1% own 40% of the World's Wealth; "Pardon".
'50% of population live on less than $2 a day!'
Life blood is Money ~ sucking your Adrenalin.
Droit de Seigneur, a mask to conceal a Slavery culture!
'Globalisation Maximizing Profits regardless of any Cost'
Brought in the Economic hit men from Houston, Texas.
Reversing sentiment ~ creating an Empire for a Shah!
"I Am .... Brain Washed"

*

<u>Created ~ Scarcity Scam!</u>
The 'Established View' fighting Progressive New Ideas!
Politics Keeping the Elite Institutions in Power – Authority!
Get down on your knees, what are your Aspirations son?
Don't want to change a Goose that gives you the Golden Eggs.
What's in it for me, Let's have Self Preservation of your Greed?
People's welfare comes second to True motive of Profiteering!
All chiseling off each other, where's the decency, humanity?
Let's have a dictatorship of the Rich over the Poor!! We do....
Set up a Covert Government serving Satan's tribe, Corruption!
You never know when the next one is coming

Easy As

"What do you do for Fun?" "Cook & Stitch" "Send her over!"
"I don't let my wife out the House" What was she wearing?
"Pain is just a registration of Life" ~ Boot's on the other foot!
She digs what is Freedom and it's enormous ~ Juicing me Om!
Absolutely, Appreciate everything you have ~ then it comes in.
Allowing gratitude, love, light, generosity, peace and harmony.
Hanging on ~ to the Love handles with some mercy.
The Universe gave me this gift ~ of life

*

Expansion Tank

"Alzheimer's the worst thing I can Imagine ~
Yeah, but you forget you got it!"
Will it set him free? From Puritanism, extremism....
Carrying his head around with him under his arm.
"My bike's completely Illegal" so is my 12 year old bride!
"It's all that queuing up for food that does it!"
'Overnight a new criminal class was created ~ Smoking a Weed!
This is how I dreamed of beautiful Goa * Free Spirit in the Tropics.
Why are we still like monkeys? There's desperate people about.
Who wants to see Tigers or Sharks eating half their own babies?
Cats eating cat; there's always the 'Odd predator' that's out there.
Funnel web's bite, a Big fucker, "Thank you & Good night!"
Evolution! Family Catastrophe!
"I don't think I'll have Religion now"
And No Propaganda… Little Jesus on Porticoes.
She's got crucifixes all over the room!
"Just want to Enjoy Life ~ who wants to go to an Asylum?

*

Quick knots ~ get out of the way

"We look for a place that was not burnt down!"
You have to come to that point because that's the way.
Integrity

Clear Clarity
Collective Consciousness ~
Switching it ~ back on
to Love, Peace and Harmony
*'One Love * One Heart'*
This was perfect love ~
A Global heart with emotional Intelligence.
Melting into the Sun.

*

Learning Languages
Walkin' on the beach ~
Viking torrents ~ Norwegian auras
Characteristics of the Northern Lights
Reflecting in her phosphor emerald pools.
"Do you want me to be your Millionaire?"
"I'm due an Excess!"
Sweet mango ~ Raw Jungle Honey!

*

Monkeylicious
Receiving messages from Outer Space made into Crop circles.
Strong connection ~ it comes, I just have to do it.
It's happening I don't like making appointments.
"Your music never lets you down Baba!"
None of the seas are as clean as they were ~
Paying for it in Langkawi ~ 'Blame it on Humans!'
"So it's War!" She threatened to come and kill me.
"Don't trouble trouble until trouble troubles you"
All 'bout the beat, "One good thing leads to another"
"They want to make you happy but they can't;
they only want to make themselves happy"
Taught to abuse those deemed
to be below them ~
Treason of a smile

<u>Beats Me</u>
I don't know what it means but I like it ~
beyond the elite, expensive world of Fine Art.
Randomly throwing together the Unexpected, instantaneous,
more beguiling, don't try and apply a Cognitive analisis,
feeling an Emotion about what can't be rationalised
Seeing through a Wrong Lens, answers, questions,
trying to Understand 'Why' is to miss the Point.....
Anything is Possible, anything goes in interior design.
Why Not, expanding Horizons; because it's Bonkers!
Just happens like everything happens ~ sensitive Egomania.
Committed a bit, have a Banana Split, he's here to learn.
Interpretation, Juxtaposition of a genome Artist ~
Imagination, innovation * of Nuclear Mysticism.
"Life is moving Atoms ~ Love is Galactic Nuclei"
'Making hay while the sun shines'
This place is unreasonable
Living in a theatrical dream...
They didn't conceive/perceive/believe
Her Cells' Organelles, DNA. are Real
*

<u>This Revolving Door</u>
LSD ~ Give it to the enemy! It came to my door!
Put it in the water supply ~ I like happy crowds.
Espousing psychedelic experience.
Using your own chemical brain
*

<u>Not thinking to Stop</u>
Enjoy yourself and things will Pop Up!
The black sheep? No, the Golden One!
'Existential has no Philosophy'
"Don't touch him he is Holy!"
It's that Simple

Dippy * Hippy

"Remembering lying in a cornfield ~
not knowing where the fuck I am in India!"
Lost in West End ~ have a bit of discipline ~ in yourself!!
Her sari thong, Lakshmi popping out of a cake! Totally devoted.
Where you goin' on your Honeymoon ~ Romantic Varanasi?
"They don't burn lepers or pregnant women ~ in the Ganges"
"½ the room was flaked out, in the Special K hole club!"
"Let's go to the beach"

*

Molecule Man

'Capitalist Human' Slogan, 'It's Good to Sweat!'
Anyone else been to bed yet? 'Arbeit macts Frei'
She's always hangin' around the Love apple tree.
He flipped out ~ admits he's been in a nut house.
There's more than the pictures, there's their meaning.
Don't want to process my visa with an imbecile!
The year after I went out with a Junkie with HIV;
I met an alcoholic with genital herpes at the corner shop!
Serenity Wrap around the Human Condition ~
You can feel the tension in the States, the vibe.
Right now my friend's expanding his 'Atman'.

*

Psychedelic Indian Myths

Patchouli Myrrh, "You stink ~ so bad ~ but I Love it"
Traveling ~ Mind Jogging, New discovery of Inner Frontier.
"If you order it here you know you're gonna eat it"
"It's OK to be stoned as long as you've got a sharp suit on, smokin'
a chillum!" Hangin' out with a lush, narcissistic, MDMA. Queen.
Saves a lot of suffering ~ you're gonna get let down.
*Gave him a Magic Pill * "Man I am a Creation*
of the Creator ~ who Created me"; "I Trust You".
"Do I have Peace?"

*Freed * OM*
Surreal {Poetic ~ Landscape, Stark Light}
An African decorated House, full abstraction.
Instinctual, Sacred Geometry ~ on their walls.
Meditation ~ dripping sweat at 5am.
"I've come to surrender!"

*

Angel Consciousness
'One man's Revolutionary is another man's Social Activist'
Their dramas on the rest of us ~Try an Energetic Therapist.
'I Fall To Pieces'
'From the battlefield of marriage'.
Born in the depths of the depression.
"I'm Crazy" ~ her signature tune.....
Sweet dreams

*

Yoga Mat ~ Goa Surfboard
Shiva Protection, Smoking for Shiva; "Bom Bolenath"
Shivaratri ~ everyone's bhanging on in their Temples!
Spaceships coming right at you! Things you don't expect.
Making Totem Poles, being on Fire, taught her about Pain.
"Please don't let it be that, Please don't let it be that, PLEASE!
You know......

*

Dating a super natural Aphrodite
I was mystified by a mystic, seduced by her cherubim mystique
What's it say about the Magi of unlocking distortions?
"I had a King Cobra in my garden in the rainy season"
*came for a frog ~ It's still alive * different dimensions.*
It's a Jungle! Massive luminous ~ jet black butterflies.
Make the bills, take the money; any more elementals?
The Inspiration around you ~ rainbow's lovely flowers.
She's a Beamer!

Spaced Shuttle
The Satellites relaying to Houston…
BIS, IMF. Wars are being Engineered ~ Inequalities on Earth!
Tories and Labour ~ dividing and Ruling ~ forever and ever.
Conquered by a debt Monetary System ~ in & out of Control!
'LSE. only a platform, it's the people who come there to Invest'
Spending billions perpetuating the Illusion, wool over the eyes.
Your greatest unbearable loss ~ Pain of devastated human hearts.
Once such beautifully peaceful people.

*

Solar * Muse
Bionic Comet in a Bright Window, full of Light ~
How can you deny it? "You can't", Naturellement.
$2 billion for one wing of a Stealth Bomber, B-2. Excoriated Spirit!
Creating a dialog between you & the object ~ However insane.
Two disparate things put together making surreal, mixed reality.
"Live or die it's up to God" *Inshallah* ~ "Que sera, sera Bella"

*

Sublime * Picasso
'Recorded the existential Carpet Bombing
of a Spanish town in a work of abstract Art'
'The Vatican's complicity with Dictatorship' Atrocity ~
"I need to take my dog for a walk to Basque country"
Believing their own Paranoia…. Is this Guernica?
Expect a War on your doorsteps, blowing up the home!
Tanks covered in blood, Stukas Attacking the factories!
The Generalissimo's men Proven on the Battlefield.
'UXB's' ~ Unexploded Bombs, in your new Cocina!
"We ran out of ammunition in the end; praise be to Jesus!"
Shell Shocked! The rampaging Holy Inquisition here again!
"They were Very Cruel, Really Cruel ~Totally without Mercy!"
Ask the Mind; Who We Are, Who I Am, what have I/we done?
What are we doing together here & now, in each other's arms?

Aut om in us * An om in us

Children had the freedom of the Prison camp!
Swerving around a holy cow, here I am now ~
Opening 'Bella Vita' ~ It's a brand New View!
There's a light from somewhere else ~ there...
Sense of another dimension ~ Projection, perception.
Seeing Planet Earth for the first time from outer space!
Beyond the normal Mind redirection ~ Self's Identification.
Opening up a Kaleidoscope, being in a Vortex, being a river.
Instantaneous Pulling from out there ~ Leaving Ego behind.
The Original push from the Heart was to get out of the Mind.
Being Universal Natural Holistic Free Infinite Spirit ~
In tune with BEYOND ~ allowing another hologram.
A glimmer of Light is everything ~ Same*Same
Something more to life, being alive effect ~
In tune with the Abstract mystic window
Let it go ~ Realising Cosmic flow

*

I Wasn't Thinking Straight

On a Crystal mission * repositivising Art, giving vibrations ~
Keeping you in tune with her ~ you wanna be fully flowing.
Deep Pink inside ~ the dog's bollocks! Potent Environments,
supports molecular flow ~ meeting people on same vibration
In the stream ~ "If ever you need an orgasm give me a ring!"
You want to be in the now tuning, be with me or Not be with me.
Energy flows ~ sucked all my juices, as dry as a raisin d'etre!
Mind loves to be distracted; Come to my World, No attachment.
Does it with a beaming smile which makes everyone Love her.
How do you understand nature? Take a trip see what happens!
Every minute you survive is a miracle ~ too much Ruling Junta!
Nice on the plateau ~ Explosions, underground Matrix energies.
'Om Mani Padma Hum'. You have to eat the shit, your shit.
To become the Lotus ~ "We're all Lovers Inside"

Swings & Roundabouts

Pros and cons 'Vigilantism with heart' Come to Save the World!
Oh Yeah, "The Eagle has landed with its ass up his head,
instead of floating on the surface of the Sea of Tranquility!"
"Going to the grave without ever having a psychedelic experience
is like going to the grave without ever having sex." Dr. Mckenna.
"Death is Fulfillment of Spiritual Life"
"Finite is here so Infinite can be felt"
"Just getting the balance right"

*

That's Perfect

"I find it really harmonic" ~ Less goin' on round about you.
Conversations with less distractions, sweeter temptations.
Happy to be keeping it easy & simple to be contented.
I'm not your Eunuch ~ born as a strong swimmer,
forever running, less dramas, liking it, energetic ~
Who wants another drama? Less Control more flow.
'If you gotta boat you're going to attract birds'
"My dick's got a brain of its own, give him a bone!"
In your comfort zone ~ "It's all good"
Infatuated by a beautiful female mirage from a distance!

*

Can you Predict it?

When it comes to Love you don't always do what you intended.
Your light is bright, will I get destroyed, burnt, needing to deflect it?
Alternative conscience ~ another state of Mind, going where?
"I trust her face, you see it, feel it, adoration in your heart"
It gets more and more clear with the Truth, let it flow freely ~
Stronger environment for Lila the better, she'll come to me.
Let's see ~ something's going on, play of energies, synergies.
Allowance, having the experience, to Love her and let her be.
When you connect inside ~ is the only place to put your Love.
It's not a game you're experiencing it, involved in your movie.

Harmonic Convergence
Facing the Plane of the galaxy ~
*The Disclosure Project * Gravity.*
Secret NASA transmissions ~
another smoking gun!
Killing to Perfection notion
*

Sharing Love
Taking the absolute vow of no absolute ~ destiny!
He gave her a perfectly balanced diamond Chakra
She gave him a beautiful ancient Jade ring ~
multi galaxies in your seeds, in your smiles
in your hearts together ~ for you both.
Betrothed to the changing moment
*

Lobster Telephone
Absurd ~ effect on your brain
The Clarity of distortions.
A new palette of sounds ~
Creating an Aria for a Soprano.
Madame Butterfly ~ who's bought himself a child bride!?
Driven by Infatuation and desire! Shall we call it Greed?
Whilst another human being's making supreme sacrifices!
Who is in Love with Love....
*

Tea is Tea
"We must not take revenge"
I will meet your spirit in the stars.
Pollen grains dancing together in spring water
Jiggling the relative nature of light ~
How many molecules in virtual particles of Shaktavara?
Sai Baba, Christ, all light workers working here right now
All working Together ~ All One

Full Visualisation
Feeling Free ~ as Air * freed*oming
Gave us the language of the imagination and unprecedented
levels of agreement close to the theory of everything ~
defining (or defying) nature on an Atomic scale....
"Empty space is seething with Activity"
Mysterious Force of streaming intergalactic photons ~
Exotic, new Creativity appearing ~ tight in a blue black dress.
Meet you at the Mars Bar sweetie.

*

Free Spirit
Mapia, Union Vegetalis #2, free as can be, fruit de Ma mere.
It's just so beautiful ~ simplicity, Colour, sweet perfumed air.
Working with frequency & metta*morphosis of 'the wild beasts'
Trees of life ~ Alive in a Naturally reflective window of effects.
Sparkling Gems, gold and turquoise generating genetic Karma.
Woke up within, glorious Dawn, inspired soul mates, entwined,
lying in a hammock by a church; why not look inside?
"They didn't get the nightmare they got the dream."

*

Releasing their Fears
Lost 90% of the Starving city of St. Petersburg to the Nazis!
"It could be me" - 20 degrees. "Thank God I'm in Bermuda!"
Earth Awakening 2012, resonance ~ renaissance, balance ~
That'll be a Party, "I'd like a Charlotte Russe, ASAP; Spasiba"
Attached to the Concept ~ of Humanity &/or Google heaven!
Putting it into Experience ~ "Just a little higher dear!"
Allowing the Heart to surf ~ the Universe

*

Pentagon Oculist
"Well I can't see any wreckage of a plane there, can you?"
Prescription ~ 'They don't want people opening their eyes'
Telling people the Truth ~ who want to believe...

Upgrade 057
A surreal mirror * became a Head.
Facet ~ nation ~ being * Yoni Altar
"Namaste", met an Indian Punk!
Everyone's on their Trip ~
Heathen ~ "I'm taking her Pain"
I Am ~ don't need to ADD anything to it.
Functioning in their Identity ~ nicer to fly!
Better if she stuck her lips on me.
Paying for a good Alibi as normal.
Sticking you up for an Easter egg!
Looking into those sultry Russian eyes
without naming it. "Privet" ~ "Spasiba"
*

Goa * Uni.
Energy orgy ~ Invaded by Peacocks!
"I'd rather do gardening ~"
They're still in there chopping!!
They're harder to deal with ~ less obedient Comrades.
Unblocking Adrenalin; Why break the Wave ~
Who wants to brake a flowing stream?
Being ONE with Life
*

21 Gms. Lighter
Bit messy Baba, calms my nerves, she drove you to cigarettes!
Resonating ART ~ recreating light and shade.
Energy On the Wall ~ Vibrations Off the Wall.
Tuning In ~ Hokusai surfing Fuji's cresting peaks.
'It doesn't exist until you see it' ~ gotta be Snappy!
3D Effects in the brain ~ Absorbing Revelation.
"All that dies is all that is not Real"
Being Aware of Awareness ~ Is being.
Super colourful reflections of the Sun

Happy Goa

Education ~"Old enough to know better"
Your connection to ~ Something Real…..
"I think my fuckin' Spleen's gone on holiday…"
Struck down ~ Need to Boost your Immune System!
"The Dalai Lama, he's my neighbour in the Mountains"
Downloading my Gallery of Fame; 'PARIS' in Hindi.
A Feast for the Eyes

*

Hippy Satyagraha

Daydreaming in Ecstasy ~ man
You practice Yoga ~ You live another life
not being Fixated ~ live and enjoy being content.
'If you say the name of the bird the child will never see the bird'
By identifying it as a 'bird' we have denied everything else it is.
"Seeing the life there in the story and Seeing yourself in it ~
Doing it for the Universe, doing everything I can"

*

FREE TO SMILE

The Power of the Dyson to alter a woman's mind!
The Power of MDMA to turn a stranger into a Minx.
Not everything has a meaning ~ a babbling brook.
I've done all that Warrior training Baba.
Driving around the World in a Psychedelic Gelateria Van.
Eureka moment ~ "Seems like an acid trip that never ended!"
*"You need another set of eyes" * "Just need to Open yours"*
The tree was dancing the whole night ~ Organic Orgasmic.
"I'm in it, do you think she's in it?" There's only so much crap
you can put up with on the way to finding something interesting.
If you have it in your consciousness ~ it happens like that!
Gurus spend their time listening to inner silence of space.
Nature telling you what's goin' on ~
Take her a Rose

We are all the Sunshine
Pantheons of light ~ Who wants to be tight, a Prick teaser?
"It could have been oh so easy, could have been me set free"
"I'm always available for you Cherie if you want to let go"
The not so nice drugs involved, fuckin' horrible delusion.
"You know, when you dread to ask!"
The Universe gave me this gift ~
Downloaded the crystals
Living in the flower of life.
*
"Get behind me Satan!"
It's complicated, complex; "The moment you give it all ~
they come back and bite you in the arse!"
Peace & Love* Open Happiness
"When you gonna grow up?"
"I am growin' ~ getting in the middle"
"Don't Identify with the beauty or you're in Pain"
"I Love it that I can still be Captivated, Seduced by her eyes"
Baba I like to be teased ~ by a sexy ADHD dream on MDMA.
Don't make yourself a slave. 'It's my life' ~ 'Live and let live!'
"The Alchemy is in the moment ~

Changing Monsoon
Water off a duck's back; 'Goa All Sorts'
Open the Fun bags ~ Dinosaurs are on their way back!
"To find the bhang you need to go to a lassi shop;
how many balls do you want?" Hangin' in the future.
Box jellyfish * on the beach
There's thousands of creatures ~
the most dangerous in the Universe!
The big fish came there to eat them.
Schools of fins living in the mangroves.
Asking yourself, "What am I doing here?"

Delusionary ELF

Hook, line & sinker, "It was possible to go to the Moon then?"
Making us think that we got a choice. Not one or the other.
Controlling the parameters, conditioning of persuasions....
Political programs of Fear, desire, Reward & punishment!
Brainwashed by the media, there is no News anymore ~
There's A I. Technology we don't know anything about.
Frying us all up with Extra low frequencies....
We're all under PsyOp attack, if you believe it.

*

Mr. Irresistible

Never lived on her roof before ~
"You gotta gorgeous arse Eve"
Needs some Shock Therapy!
Then I found an Apsara ~ in the nude.
An Asteroid Belt in her head

*

Spicy Kali

Invite her over for a Shepherd's Pie ~
In love with a lunatic, at a Space party.
"All is possible, is it probable?"
She's fully tattooed up ~ house next to a Vortex.
Keep 'em smiling and yu got no problems.
Solar flares, mass confusion, time bombs.
We need a change ~ try a Bombay divorcee!

*

Gaia

Fully absorbed together.
Give her a Hologram
Give her a Caravan, stick her in the garden.
Going to work on a Rollercoaster.
6' 2" & Buxom ~ "Who Wants Fun?"
Opening up a Full gusher

<u>Critical Mental Development</u>
"It's the Thought that counts" * Find a Solution
to what leaves a Karmic seed growing into fruit ~
Blooming in your being ~ Who do you want to be?
Take Greed and Only Money view out of the equation, left with
Different Behavior ~ Read the Dhammapada, the Lotus Sutra.
Can you Imagine Loving Yourself before you Love another?
If You have hate for someone, you'll carry that hate inside you;
Deprivation, Scarcity, Poverty, Crime, effecting the Sublime.
Free All Life Force from Living out existence in total servitude.
Machines taking over, sooner the better feel divine frequency
FREE TIME
*

<u>Common Good</u>
Scarcity increases Profit where is the human incentive biased?
Have a Greenback, the President Kennedy debt Free currency!
Otherwise we're all working and paying taxes to the Banksters!
How's it feel to be a Modern Slave? How's it feel to starve son?
Gave Unrepayable loans to developing populations' despots.
Good ol' Corporatcratic hitman, back again on their behalf.
Sign this Agreement of 'Indentured Servitude' or Else!
'Invisible' Economic Warfare, perpetrated on y/our children!
March of the Conglomerates running the World ~ Consequences.
Scientifically engineering the next Global Financial Collapse!
*

<u>The Hook</u>
Singing avocados… Don't fall ~ In Love!
What is Love? The First Look ~ Really beautiful.
Might be a raving lunatic ~ triggered something
maybe I need a few Extra complications!
Even when the Sun goes down it'll be back.
A Passion Collision ~ in a field of sunny haystacks.
Feeling her reaction; I want to feel Wanted ~ a lot Stronger!

Erotic Pie
Hip Sugar daddy, Raw demerara
High cream Cheeks ~ Potlatch
Receiving Venus'
flowing lovely Inspiration
*

"I love the name Venus"
Awareness of Sensation flowing ~ upstream
Let it go ~ less memory ~ Being as it is
Activating the Hemispheres ~ Conjugal bliss
'Everyone's High on Sky' (slogan)
Tuning into ~ 'The Open Prana Channel'
*

Pulsating Viral
Had a Stroke ~
tight in my heart.
Virile Pagan Pan
Had a Big Erection
for fecund Pachimama
triggering Pollination
Osmosis of the Vital ~ Mind
*

'Hi Normal'
Sitting on a Mountain holding blue crystals and chanting Om.
The Ashram Escape experience ~ Living it freely.
The bottom line is ~ don't drive Insane thru Pain
being sub atomic ~ ripples in the Universe.
Brilliant Mirrors and Reflections ~ No words.
Hooked in a city; a rat with its favorite cheese.
Being used – hanging to Serve What/Whom?
"How the fuck did I end up in this?"
"Up to our neck in shit Terrorism!"
Live stock ~ Remote Controller

Obsesssional Insanity

No Controlling You ~ caught with a hook in your back!
Ethereally and other dimensions.
'Miners don't get claustrophobic'
"I don't believe in going back over old bridges"
You should have a 'Party' Award!
Cocaine Management, no borders.
"I don't give a fuck, you get
the most out of Life that's there"
Don't close your Mind to anything ~ took off the blinkers.
Best Advice formula ~ synthesising the molecule MDMA;
Ecstasy when you're having a great time on the chemicals.
Psycho Pharmacology, psycho actives that alter Your Mind.
Helps dissolving barriers ~ reducing fear, lessening PTSD.
Torturers on the loose and 'Extraordinary Renditionings'.
What's justice got to do with it? Ask the Hypocrisy Minister!
Pills flooding ~ so good brought in the 'Emergency Powers'
Authority that did all they could to STOP everything flowing

*

Ringing Wet Paradigm

"Conscious raising ~ something to hit and get the beat"
Mandalas <:> What is a dimension? Be instant Space ~
Are we in the same flow sweetheart? "Chello without choice."
Hippy is just sharing ~ Sex, drugs, Rock & Roll for Rock Stars!
Building walls and boxes in the brain ~ turn it off from feeding.
Better not take any of their Fork-tongued Information Programs.
Who's following your Orders? Choosing puts you in the Game.
'You come to the top of the ladder then there's nowhere to go'
Cracking the enticing Siberian Code for a foreign love affair ~
No Expectation. Fully lock & Loaded, with her own chemicals!
"Time is your handcuff, the brain is your cell"
'Not my problem, no patterns, be creative, find a solution'
More freer

<u>New Energy ~ Feedback</u>
Existing Bio*logical Intention ~ Goddess Eve
Star seed spirals throughout the Love channels.
"The Earth is the Lord's and the fullness thereof"
Inscribed on the Facade of the Mansion House.
What's it really mean Baron? Where's the Chemical balance?

*

Separation ~ intuition ~ return to existence
burning another paradigm on the Ghats.
Trackers assessing the resonance ~
"Where do you come from my Cherie?"
Where are we going & Who are you mate?
Flowing through the Quantum Temple Gate ~
Keep it Real, keep it True, keep it Crystal clear dear.
Not given a Mind Desensitised to Full 'Collateral damage' yet!
Synergetic blooming, symbiotic lotuses ~ Zero point Processes

*

<u>Gone with the Wind to 'Gitmo'</u>
President George Bush Pardoned himself from Responsibility!
All his Administration got Immunity; Enemy non – combatants'
lost hearts & minds; another big whitewash at the White House!
No Officer was convicted from the Army Interrogation School.
Perpetuating the Legalised Abuse; What about the Victims?
How about our Principles, Senior leadership's Intentions, humility?
Two wrongs, how to make them right? No Sanctity, human dignity,
never tried to be the good guys, destroyed my Faith in Justice.

*

<u>A Privilege to live in Camp 4</u>
Wednesday get cake, Pepsi on Monday, what's the real thing?
Product placement, PR. Stunts at Guantanamo's Gift Shop!
Ask yourself if you're CRAZY! Abandoned Camp X Ray!
Camp 5 > 24 hour confinement in an 8x5 feet cell from hell.
Is there anyone a sense if this will ever END? REDACTED!

Enceladus' Light Bomb!
The most reflected object in the Solar system
The sound of clogs clattering down the road...
Ecstatic orgasmic, oceanic ~ Counter Intelligence
The White ladies blowing kisses to the firing squad.
Seductress on the Front line fighting for a cause she believed in,
not for the faint hearted ~ "People being afraid of other people!"

*

Think Tanks

Bureaucracy: justify your Job; Where's the Results we wanted?
Nature in action ~ in human Form. Decoding how we see reality.
His 'Unilateral Invasion' justification, UN still says it's illegal!
Justified, He admitted that to get rid of the tyrant was enough;
China says the same about their theocratic terrorist Dalai Lama!
"Let's get rid of our enemy and take 100,000 civilians with 'em."
Demolished International Law, makes 'em War Criminals folks!
Intervention, Preemptive Attack, excuse of every tin pot Despot.

*

Dropping the Movie!

She has a Scorpio Moon; He's a triple Taurus.
Singing ~ 'Angels without wings'
'Serenity' ~ The Privileged of the Earth, having free time ~
It's changing ~ broke the fuckin' Atlantic Conveyor belt!
'Finding the Extraordinary in the ordinary'
"We Killed All the Fish, Sorry"
Let it unfold ~ nonstop!

*

Universal Gypsy

Raw chocolate chillums, Lemon Acid, peyote sausages,
Psilocybin sprays. Can see she's becoming Conscious ~
Fear from helplessness ~ bubbles in bubbles, bursting, Pop!
*Everything & nothing in the Zazen garden * Smoke It & Eat It.*
"Hallo Autumn leaves" ~ blowing In Lak'ech's net

63

Keep A Secret
"Story of a looney, twisted gay kid...
Ran away to Afghanistan became a Taliban!
You couldn't make it up.....
Cross Pollinated, deep into being dominated
by some Tribal Lord fantasy; wants to ravish him!
Brought up in a female scented house ~
"She is very special, he is the most special!"
"Thick as pig shit and worked as a fish cook.
He's just psychotic, going up the wall....."

*

Introspective * Happiness
Interpreting the visual languages of the World ~
Notion of Paranoia, let the rocks suggest something.
Choosing ~ 'Can't show them something that they can't see.'
Expressing himself with Impunity ~ discovering surreal sub conscious
Poetry of wild flowers

*

(Being ~ Occupied)
'The Weeping Woman' ~ Portraits seen from Parallel Universes.
Made a sketch of her being ravaged by a Minotaur in full heat!
Having respect for your compagnon, beside you through a War;
whilst being motivated to paint Nazi aerial bombing; Genocide!
Holding your hand, being your Mistress, being your friend too.
Did you forget so easily ~ your sacred Muse?

*

Nenuphar * Meditation
The chillum was doing a figure of 8 ~
Then you went into another consciousness.
Closed down the Mind
Ecstasy ~ Opened up
the Creative flow ~
Pure Juiciness

Goa Time

Swinging in all directions ~ without doing calculations!
"Dropping Bombs ~ felt a slight shudder in his wings"
She's a Bombay wallah girl, he's a whirling Dervish.
Reprogramming ~ Love is second to your devotion.
Just the trauma was enough!

*

Sparkling * Diamonds

4th generation Unemployed…
"I'd like to get a crystal chandelier"
"We got the best chandelier in the World,
Stars in the sky every night"
The Higher Consciousness

*

My Peacock

If you get tight ~
You get the connection
Everything fits ~
They let you into their little Conch.
Definitely, Yes, Maybe ~
Bamboo massage every day!
Where is the Sun?
What the Fuck!

*

Free Hand

*A Real Artist * Pixels by Pixies ~*
Secrets hidden inside the cabinet.
"What the fuck is an Aperitivo?"
'Smoking Stunts Your Growth!'
"What you doin' here if yu don't take drugs?"
You see things & ask why I dream of things & ask why not?
Corrupt Religion got in the way of the stars..
"My body is feeling you!"

Virtually Flirting
Picking up Greed at the corner shop
Redesigning a way to Free humanity.
Then let's have some Intelligent ~
Management of the Planet's resources.
'Scarcity keeps products valuable, the 'Interest' Debasing LIFE!
Perpetual debt banging down your door! More money there is
the More Debt there is, the More money there is; Ad infinitum!
'Living off the wobbly benefits of a Clandestine Empire'
Vampires Diminishing the Power of people.
"He wouldn't allow himself to be corrupted"
*

The Blood Sacrifice - of the Emperor
'I don't give a fuck about their Mental states'
"It's only we who got them off the coke and onto MDMA"
She liked to spike herself with Rohypnol! Why burn the Yacht?
CorporatoCrazy Venezuela keep Pumpin Oil for US. Por Favor!
Who is running Your Life? BIS. World Bank, IMF; eating you all up.
Blowing up in 45 mins! Let's Open another children's Sweatshop!
Let's have some more cruel Environmental Destruction, Exploiters!
Greedy Profiteering, Preserving Conglomerate, Capital Elites.
Using sinister Counter Terrorism as a Tool of Fear and Power!
So people will have to fight each other to Survive ~ Status Quo.
Let's change ~ and listen to Jacque Fresco at the Venus Project.
*

Quasi Police State
Thank God for squats ~
Thank God for rave parties.
"What's the point of it all going up and down ~
If there's no one there to take it in?" Knowing it ~ Inside Out!
'The cats in boxes' theory, query. Give it space to fall apart ~
Don't be attached, eating & digesting the shit for themselves.
'Make Love not War' tattooed on his back, over the rainbow ~

<u>Design Your Day</u>
Islamic Fashion ~ 'Agent Provocatrice'.
The Hijab Collection * being Anonymous.
Lucid dreaming ~ the Illusion ~ soaring Alar.
'There is no Separation between things' Inshallah!
"Wake up and smell the coffee, see any value in it?"
Where's the Off switch? Slow it down, Pause, reboot.
Keep it going ~ Happy Party ~ "Life is a dance floor ~
if you got music in your head you dance anywhere"
*

<u>The Perfect Bean</u>
Born out of light energy ~ picked some Celandine.
Putting the whole spectrum together to make light.
"You got distracted!!!!" * "If it's comin' I'll have it."
At least enjoy your life as much as possible.
It's a coffle, slave market not a black market!
Ocean Flowers blooming on the full moon ~
being blessed by crystal clear Finnish women.
*

<u>Amazon Cloud</u>
Between the Delta theta wave ~
Get in the groove, dropping into Space.
No boundaries ~ give it up, go out of the wanting
then you can have it ~ (has anyone tried this at home?)
The Perfect Match ~ is Inside you
Flowing out ~ flowing in and out.
Perfect in our Imperfection
*

<u>Willing Chilling</u>
"A dog needs a Master and a cat has slaves"
"It's gone off what do I do?"
"Self-destructing!"
"You're worth It"

<u>"I am loving it"</u>

'Able to change your life!' "How can You change life?"

Life is Life

People think Love is desire, wanting or expecting ~

"You can change your mind"

Love is Oneness

"Recognising what you are as everything else"

Serotonin, some people always have a fixed grin!

Now I'm happy with raw chocolate ~ a Great High!

About what's goin' on in the brain! Y/ours & theirs!

Need a couple of devotees.

*

<u>Ergot Baguettes</u>

Acid crystals between the joints!

A live vortex ~ spinning Spiral Mandalas

Changing Time ~ Space * Sacred geometry.

Fearful of your Reptilian brain arising…

Terrorizing, dominating, aggressivity!

Eye of the Milky way resonating ~

frequency all round the Universes.

*

<u>A Process</u>

We're All doomed by Judgment!

We're Atomic bomblets going off ~

Blue banded Serpents of a Binary Star.

Very switched on ~ Anti Babylon.

Literally running for your life!

LSD molecules and brain hormones.

Firing rockets through the synapses…

embracing more of the natural high ~ No Time.

Inhibitor boosters stopping other Tryptamines

circulating a lot more Serotonin light!

Who wants to go to sleep?

Hallucinating Psychedelic Space

"40 hours on Meow, thought it was the drugs, it was Swine flu!"
She got her period, that old chestnut! "¼ a day is an enhancer."
*"I use the drugs to entertain myself" * 'Acid stays Boss' ~*
"Nothing wrong with this Coke she just took too much, flipout,
unbelievable, what a twat!" "They've dabbed that bag clean!"
Anaesthetized myself on Ephedrine when lovely nymphs walked in!
Kabbalah for Dummies ~ the real artist comes out in the moment!
"Emptiness ~ eh, don't be frightened Baba" Can you lose rain ~
you can't lose anything can you? It transmutes, forever now ~
Too much time on your mind, lying in a ditch staring at the Moon!
Grey cells have gone ballistic in a kaleidoscopic camouflage suit!
The sea moves the wind ~ living under a Killer bees' hive, bewitched.

*

Healing * Feeling

Honey's massage ~
Labia licking good.
Downloading

*

Love En*ergy * Rela*tivity Split

Having quiet time with your woman ~ a girl with an Italian chillum!
Her energized crystal dildos, many different ways to communicate.
She took another stream ~ dreamt a completely different dream.
Had to let her go ~ lovely to meet you, what do we ever know?
Seducing You, falling into MDMA infatuation's big violet eyes.
You Weren't FEELING It ~ Are You BEGINNING To FEEL It now?
Looking in the wrong direction, try a new transcendental Orientation.
He's vulnerable too, she just kept feeding him ecstatic, dripping drops!
Full set of sequences ~ sparkling, friendly, High octave, Open smile ~
Sorted it out in my heart and head. I wasn't listening to what she said.
Barking up the wrong tree! Rejection, Instant dismissal, felt released.
Mate how do I still go Happy with the flow, tangoed with our Ego?
It's her allowance as a free spirit

<u>Know your Acid, Bombs, Chillums, Drug Dealers</u>
Responding to a serious emotional breakdown ~
What sort of dosage you give to the experience!
So not an Overload ~ don't hold back with anything.
Don't be an unfortunately, Live yourself Authentically
Even with your own Big Shit!
Learning Process ~ Full Shakti Power
waking up the old Shiva.
Just under the skin ~ highest Concentration
of her hot compounds.
You peel it off.
*

<u>Our Dearest Masters</u>
Karmic cameras to make you feel uncomfortable, begin Paranoia.
Diabolical ~ Scaring a 4 year old to death and tapping her blood!
Rich in Endorphins ~ who's worshipping the demon?
More twisted ~ the best drug available to Satan!
Full Feed Love ~ bring them over their evil ritual.
*

<u>Perception by Design</u>
'Give them the picture you want them to see, to LOVE you ~
They go in the clichés and make the underlying Patterns of Fear,
Control, subjugation, brain washing, Keeps you from being FREE.
Totally distorted puts you in an emotional hang-up, of turmoil.
Some let themselves be manipulated.
You either want it or you don't want it ~
That one from Belarus who was looking deeply into my eyes.
**

Allow the New Age World, New Paradigms to unfold through us.
"If you want to Open yourself up, it's what you're calling in"
Innumerable explanations ~ Live our own beingness
Inside ourselves see the Innocence.
"I live as a Gaia naturist"

Poetry *Revolutionary* Art

"Like a cuppa tea?" "I got the kettle on" doesn't need meaning.
Variety of Complications ~ Lions licking their lips with a growl.
Good choice, yeah on reflection! 'Look back and turn to salt!'
Breathing up the energy from the ground ~ We're living proof.
"I never want to have to Lie." Who is the Ultimate Predator?
"If you can't give everyone a fruit & nut bar what's the point"
That's the World I want to live in ~ simply sharing a joint!
"It's about everyone becoming HAPPY"
Gaia embracing Quantum Universes

*

Juicing Mescaline

All the alkaloids existing in a small love potion * Ananda Mind.
More neurotransmitters ~ more in the moment, no tomorrows.
MOA. inhibitors making you live innocently as a child inside.
If you stop the thinking Mind, left with Cosmic Awareness ~
Try a Saffron Chocolate Bar, she's the magic Queen of herbals.
Stamen of the Crocus, strongest hybrid of San Pedro's Cactus,
and a nice collection of buttons.

*

Organic Structure

Full streaming ahead ~ flowing juicy Yoni
Together ~ s/he's in the love field; I never saw that coming!
"I'm feeling pure female Shakti, baba!" She's superb.
"I'm not your human, emotional, fetish dildo darling"
"Why do you have to go somewhere to meditate ~
Isn't it about what's goin' on inside you anyway?"
"Could have sat at home and saved a journey"
Meditation is an excuse, be here right now!
You can only be in meditation
Can't provoke it Guru ~ state of being Yourself.
Matter of Allowance ~ feeling heart's frequency.
Really surprised at her super natural beingness

Quantum * Kaleidoscope

Silence is the most beautiful music, multi-dimensional streaming.
*Intersecting with our reality * it is pretty trippy.*
Vomiting like a demon, you'll all get a bucket!
Catching a fly with chopsticks, playing table tennis with nun-chucks!
*Being Zen * infinite reality ~ all Aliens travelling in virtual Space-ships.*
*As a person because we imagine who we are * missing who we Really are!*
*Same programming from a deeper plane * It's gotta come out somewhere ~*
The Matrix's web been here from the beginning of time evolving each instant.
10% mind, 90% nature, fine tuning super-volcanoes, transformation, embrace it.
*'Where there is sweetness there are ants * law of nature'*

*

Daoist *Kamalaksa* Lotus eyes

Miracles ~ to get the blessing ~ is more than the Matter.
If you don't know you accept it fully, trusting you darling.
In lust with a Demimondaine ~ Relinquishing Yourself
falling in the Higher Self ~ encompassing the whole.
"It can be what you want it to be" Discernment ~
No more Schizophrenic structures ~ Set it Free.
Images, "Is there any Judgment to be made?"
Two circles evolving Your Individual Kundalini
flowing from the 4th dimensional heart charka.
Don't be too strong with your unique holistic Self.
Demons Inside ~ Freundlich mit your dark side!
Devilish, living through a mirror ~ Feed it, Love him
and make him a good friend, then he has No Power!
*Care for Your Cosmic being*with deep compassion.*
Allowing ~ it all to happen not being in total Control!
Road trip to Varanasi, don't get out the Spaceship.
You get out there's troubles! You're helpless ~
It works at all Altitudes

I'm enjoying it
Let's experience it ~ otherwise what's it all about?
You can fuck your own Rampant Rabbit!
I don't wanna Stop something like that,
not caught up making them understand.
Why would you block the natural Sex flow?
Frightened by the emotions of falling in Love ~
Off the edge into something unknown & DEEPER!
Might be afraid of flying ~ Not afraid of Loving You.
Happy inside your stream ~ without any Promises.
Who's gonna want...? "I want to be swept away"
The Consequences ~ of a Lover giving you Pain!

*

Are you Venus' Virus?
"I thought about that 30 years ago, seeing beauty on drugs!"
It doesn't matter, who cares? Be in this moment now ~
Angels in disguise, melting hearts of women....
"So what shall I do with my brain, give it to you?"
We Love the Mind, shows Ego how to be Mindful.
'The deepness of the voice'
Greed or the Sunshine ~

*

Happy with Rejection!
"I've seen God, yeah a part of God!"
Gurus living in a Crystal Temple,
fish jumping in the Pacific Ocean ~
All in a Trance ~ simpler the better.
Venus in Scorpio, this is Lovely!
"Anybody got a skin I can borrow?"
Raw Chocolate the right Sacrament.
Bhang Lassi is a very good toxic cleanser.
Flirting Black Angels from Frankfurt, craving reflections.
'Inviting attention merely for amusement' ~ What is real?

S21 Bus & Our Public Servants

'The wise lament neither for the living or the dead' ~Bhagavad Gita, Ch.2.11.
Expect nothing and everything is good enjoying the completely unexpected.
Reflecting it for You; a Gift for going through with it ~ basically your fine tuning.
We're all being led around by the nose into the Killing Fields, fully hypnotised!
'Trespassers will be executed' stay in the shade darling.
"I know what the Law is and it's on my side... I am FREE
It's Your World Not their World, you can do anything you want.
Claim your life otherwise they will. No joinder, 'I am signing this under duress!'
Statutes and Regulations are being used to abuse you of your natural rights!
"Have I committed a crime, broken any natural Not commercial law officer?"
"You've taken an Oath, your duties and responsibilities to protect my rights"
A deception, stopped unlawfully by PC. Plod who has No jurisdiction.
You gotta stand up for your rights as a King. 'As God is my witness!'

*

Wooed Uncut

Manifesting of light ~ She Sparkles now!
Kiss the feet of the woman and be happy Mr. Cuddles.
There is nothing external, experience every kind of stage.
"Gold is helping you feel connected to the Sun, for Self esteem,
Silver is Integration." Layers of minerals, all the elementals Inside.
You create your own reality ~ try some Energetic Lila Play!
"Nothing happening anyhow on the Still Point of the stream"
The greedy Mind wants more, more instead of giving more!
In answer to your prayer, in answer to your-self,
in answer to your heart ~ Rare empathetic Earth

*

Cocky Funny

A numbers game ~ Who am I gonna be today?
Go as far as you want to go ~ in the Allowance.
The bubbles could get a bit messy! Can't argue with that!
"There's none so blind as those who will not see"
Choosing Ambient chill, Techno but Psychedelic Trance ~
brings me closer into the moment ~ nothing to lose anyway

"On your bike
~ take yu balls and sling ya fuckin' hook!"
The Divorcees Gift ~ 'Your Scrotum Jewelled Parure!'
A set of embossed Golden plated bollocks dangling from
her diamond necklace with a giant 24 carat ring and chain!
*Kali's * Self Empowerment ~ In Ekstasis.*

*

Recycled bullock's cuff-links
Mixing ~ The Best of Everything
*Life goes on * Existence takes care of it*self*
"I had a bad Prawn"
"There's a lot to be said for Paganism"
Being bit more Psychedelic ~

*

Going Up Line
"She put lips on me" ~ melted in her arms,
becoming enlightened on raw chocolate!
'Death is the fulfillment of Spiritual life'
Burn the letters.......

*

Critical Tigris
*Sublime Lila ~ Feeds the Inside*out with a smile.*
Feels like I'm now living in a Quantum Spaceship.
Iraq - do your thing, "Hey Man, Peace, Salam"
"I just Shantied it"

*

Star Consciousness
*Lotus Jewel * Heart Jewel * Lotus Star*
*Lotus Heart * Heart Star * Star Jewel*
Gotta shut the mind up ~ "I'm not your castrated Eunuch mate!"
Getting the lust back Baba; You see that behaviour as normal?
Can't be any limited mind-thoughts ~ Planting the living Seed.
*It's not in only Survival * It's life.....*

She Is Shamanic

She is a Tantra Magician, she's an Aphrodisiac delusion.
Dancing is the World's rhythm expressing itself ~
Concrete Jungle ~ I'm a Shiva Valley Sannyasin.
Own Lucky Charm ~ We are our Image Mirage
7 chilies and a Lemon to keep the demons away!
Miracles are there to be claimed ~
Sitting with the horny, jungley Babas

*

Mr. Grumpy's Chattels

All a lot of shit happened to me ~ Lost it all!
"Not a headache, I call it a learning experience."
He'll never change his Spots ~ down at the Oasis.
We all Want to Be Loved ~ Full Recovery in process.
Love is this strange Cocktail mix ~ see what happens
Not making it happen ~ Letting Love happen.

*

Keep it Fluid

"I Love those Juxtapositions of Character!" Showed me the beast!
But when one will do something you've never seen before!
It had a very large hood, gorgeous! Still erupting, she's a Bullfighter
in full heat! I'm not gonna get into dramas ~ famous last words!

*

Twinkling Comet

Full on Cosmic Explosion ~ can't argue with that!
Fully impregnated ~ integrated with fecund nature.
Nothing more fertile than a hot Orgasmic woman!
"Don't bring your bollocks to other people's houses"
"Too much negative vibe, if you talk shit, shit happens"
Celebrating Life is Spiritual ~ Making Shanti feelings.
Pachamama dancing at the Carnivale ~ Look up, Go up!
"I've got a girlfriend in Italy who plays the accordion for me"
'Coquette' ~ a bird who loves Coke!

Chillum Friendly

After 3 chillums and 2 cocktails!
All about the Stars * Goa addict ~
Checking for a pulse ~ got to the other side,
went to live by the beach in natural Agonda.
"She'll end up playing you again"
Swimming with all her clothes on.
Being chased by a gigantesque Tsunami ~
All living on the razor's edge man ~ Faster faster!
Don't need the new wife to do Puja every morning ~
before I leave the house, unless she's a Persian Sufi!
Losing the Plot ~ each one's unique destiny is to enjoy.

*

It is as it is ~ Isn't it

"I'd like to be your best Mate but it's not the right time" ~ Oh soul!
Gotta Centre myself to be Free, to feel her ~ let's have FUN.
Saves a lot of Suffering ~ "you're gonna get let down again!"
Becoming more & more normal ~ missing the colourful people.
Been down that road before… Head full of Vanity.
I don't regret havin' her tattoos on me.
Making a Daoist Peacock for my-self.

*

Skanky Bimbo Barbie

25 chillums before I left the Temple! Opportunity with the acid.
"Afforded ourselves the luxury of being timeless-observers"
She just wants to do what!!!? Why not?
Goose pimples under her light Sundress.
What have I done?

*

Tosh Wallah

Still travellin' from 'ere to 'ere ~
"I went trekking in the Himalayas with the Dalai Lama"
"That's nice son, did you see Pop Idol?"

8 Miles to 9

Classified Illegal ~ "If yu got em you might as well drop em!"
Eco Activist and Shanti hippie, chilling at Nirvana, Nagarkot,
Sitting, smoking chillums, looking at the Magical Himalayas.
'A good girl gonna go bad' ~ lotta eye candy out there.
Energetic sperm ~ ecstasy in a valley of sunlit blisses.
You shot she fell!
Playing with fluffy peaks, her kisses.
No drugs just Crystals and rainbows.
"Don't fart in your own Spacesuit"
Stag Night ~ tried to grab a whore!
Not a good idea, powders on the lawn.
'Nobody is Imperfect ~ In the Perfection'
The whole thing's a Program downloaded to your brain.
It's Art creating Reality < TV > Online keys into your Mind!
"Natural beauty, a fabulous body, I'd eat that Alive!"
'We can share because we care'

*

Tantric Baba * Tantra Wallah

"Thank you for making me dream"
"All this External is coming from Inside You"
On a very real Level this doesn't exist.
Mutual Attraction ~ feeling the bliss

*

4 Original Sin

Unbelievable the way they Persecute humanity!
He's looking for something to fulfill that female side.
At a Psychedelic Party dancing with a Chadian Sorceress.
Inner State of Bliss ~ in your gleaming smile.
Revealing more this Aspect of My character.
You're ramping up the Passion; "I want your Orgasms!"
It's a Mind Game ~ Hypnotised by a fantastic femme fatale.
"They plough their women!" ~ PUA 101, Online

Free Inside

Direction > *"The more you love the more love you get back"*
"When 23 chromosomes come and meet and have this dance ~"
Flow of Chaos between us, need Consciousness flowing freely.
On the same wavelength ~ or not?
Overpowering moments ~
Your energy is very spaced out ~ putting it more into the centre.
Focus it on those you love ~ And who love you & be Universal.
She wants to be transmuted ~ "I'll be round in half an hour".
"It's when I need to be locked in my flat & take these Big Pills!"
And know we go UP and have a synergetic journey.
Rationing organic ~ nature forever filling in the gaps

*

Mussolini, Fellini, Pasolini!

"I'm lookin' for Escapism"
You take from the hug ~
She's in a changing process like everyone else.
You respond to the hug in ease and Love it.
"Come around for a chillum ~ It is as it is, it must be.
No more suffering, we work with that ~
Caressing your breasts anti-clockwise
And keep those lips close to me!

*

Sooner

We'll all be eating Dim Sun.
We'll be eating each other!
Work building another Network, trusting his intention.
We hold the strings ~ completely different Job descriptions.
Now unfolding of its own accord
"Don't want to get in the way of true Majesty"
Back to the Circle ~ Energy has lots of games!
*Aligning the female * manifesting Life Forms.*
"We are the Honey"

Fuchsia * Soleil

In that Golden Light *Yeah on reflection* "It happened to me."
"So wrong but it's right!"
"I can feel You ~ Can you feel me?" Look into my shining eyes.
Carrying her personal dildo, chillum bag, 'av a dab dab!'
Big Joint in the Sky ~ I'm in the Sunshine Tribe.
White gold, peachy saffron my favourite colour.
Can't complain ~ staying in a Palace!
So many Light*Minded people sharing.
Can't say No, why say No? Why not?
"I met the junior Madam, she's ringing wet"
Fulfilling ~ A smile inside

*

Anti-Personnel

Worse than making an infestation of Cobras in your town!
Skulls & Crossbones, Danger of Death, Beware our Mines!
Outside Shit Rock reality; Always nice to see a dolphin ~
"I believe in Myself, I am a God; We're all Gods Baba"
"Not enough people throwing bricks through turrets!"
The Game of Life

*

Spin Out

It's more than any coincidence ~
There's a Pagan Temple vibrating off Junction 9.
Working at my Optimum * a heat seeking Missile!
No Danger

*

White Hot!

Sucking it in & see ~ Goa can be an innovative global Interface.
Stepping back from your flame otherwise I'll get fuckin' burnt!
You have to give it the Space to fall into place ~ no Expectation
'Seva' Joy ~ 'doing it in an Unconditional love direction'
Perfect Child * "I love this little human"

80

Puking up her ankles
Only liquid goes with the flow ~Tryin' to suck it Up!
"I AM the Captain of this ship of light * Welcome"
Beautiful experiences making her heart glow ~
"He didn't have any reason to doubt her honesty ~
and she was accepted by all the Psychedelic people"
It's the washout of the bottle!
Acid called Crystal Clarity.
"Sometimes the walk back was better than the Party!"
Why did you rob that bank? My Guru told me ~
"I'll appeal to the Universe"
*

Alchemic Land
It's a Gateway Goa and you gotta go there.
The Magick hasn't finished ~ Instant, in tune.
Tantra Academies popping up all over Anjuna!
"She melt me like crazy, she's a dream chocolate."
"Love can happen in seconds, forgiveness takes a lifetime"
Being in the Temple of Love ~ Spying in the Theatre of passionate lust.
Ascending her heaving Vulva mountain, free falling down the other side.
*

Violet is the shortest wave
Vegetalis ~ Fresh from Peru!
Gifts of a Tantric Highlight tribe.
Giving their children Sacred Tea.
Living with the Plants * Alive.
She is bringing you onto the Ayahuasca frequency ~
Showing you all the Spaces ~ Seeing the whole Crystal.
You are; and see how much harm you have given yourself!
All the Banana bullshit ~ giving you all the Illusions of reality.
Working on Your Self, having your own Experience.
Holding yourself ~ Allowing yourself to Reconnect.
Contemplate, "You don't look in other people's eyes"

A Life Model
He'll do the Hula Hoop, throw a Frisbee.
See what happens ~ A tension!
"When the music is no more the player"
The Taurus dancing with the Scorpion!
Deep but Up ~ No buts……..

*

Party Room
'Rent a Puja' ~ in a luxury Limousine!
PSYCHEDELIC * C L A S S I F I E D S
'When all the birds are singing in the sky'.
'Love Is In The Air'
'Love Is Everywhere'
'Love Is All Around'

*

Today Rolling!
Big softy in Electric Ladyland.
"One day you're going to die"
The Biggest Secret > Consciously!
In between we have Fun.
Why not?
The Cosmic University of laughter.
Getting the blood tests ~ frequency.
It's not a doing it's tuning into Space.
Letting your Mind go astray ~
Not being its servant but the Maestro.
Body & Mind in synch with the heart beat
Not thinking ~ Feeling the Celestial song.
Allowing it to appear in alignment ~
if you don't put yourself in your own way.
Acceptance of the contradictions, exactly here.
You call Angels or demons, it's up to you ~
"Too hot to Stop!"

Super Explosion

Scared to like it, or there's a lot more fishes in the sea!
You want ALL that Power for You, for your own reflection.
She's carried away, her ego's more Shanti.
'The Greatest Pleasure Is To Give Pleasure'
"I want to be with someone who wants to be with me"
"I know how it feels" ~ Putting it off as long as you could.
If I don't get enough to feel it then not enough to give it back!
Soul has no Age, it's your Experience ~ experiences you like.
"I don't like those Power trips ~ I want to be free flowing baby"
Feeling the movement ~ Venus ejecting Mars' imploding stars!
Lost in each other's Orgasmic grip.....

*

Free to Me

Free as part of this channel ~ "I'm only seeing it Wide OPEN"
In UK there's a Law Controlling ~ the flow ~ to Stop it, Why?
"I would have dived for it myself but I was too reclined"
You can undo it as much as you can do it ~ visceral.
Because it's a reflection ~ gossamer, ethereal.
The Grateful Dead have got a lot to answer for....
Good news from America, Hippies are Alive & thriving in NYC.
Contemplating * It's all an Illusion ~ embracing Noh dancing.

*

100%* Elemental * Chemical *Zero Point

"Your ship's come in" * "that's what I think,
right on me harbour ~ on me river boat."
"When I die I go back into the Universe"
'This thing that gets up & moves around'
That's what a feeling is, isn't it?
Earth is a Brain ~ Coordinating physical and mental action.
'My chemical reaction attracted to your chemical reaction'
Now we're in a multi*dimensional flow ~ are you feeling it?
Yin & Yang ~ Same*Same, dark energy enlivened Space.

Nepali Trekking!
He just calls it walking
walking to his village ~
Have to walk 3 days after the bus.
*

Baby Chillum
Inside a Living Ashram, front of the yellow house by the ocean.
Early Qi Gong at the Secret beach and knitting by candlelight!
"It's an Art to work without electricity in Modern times"
"Warum nicht?" ~ 'Variety is the Spiiiiiiicccccccce of Life'
If you go there he will rebuild you ~ "I'll rebuild myself"
In real life ~ a beautiful Space close to a Solar Pagoda.
Tempting a Black Goddess ~ Lost in ultimate Chaos
*

Daoist everything
Super dangerous mango seeds, strawberries and grapes!
Nature's Self-sufficiency ~ What to do? Get your own tree…
*

Stuck inside the Pipe
"Coke puts me to sleep ~ shuts me up." All about the Attention!
Addicted to Pain Killers, try Arnica, Anti-Codex, alternatives!
Protecting white Poppy fields, purifying it once for Morphine.
'If you own the Opium you own the Pharmaceutical World'
Something to STOP your Agony! 'Om Mani Padma Hum'
Love as evil as a Viper ~ She came to Goa gave up Prozac!
'All the red hot girls are on Ketamine and the socializing drug,
where you never tell the truth, built on lies' ~ "I feel decadent!"
She's wonderfully speedy enough to keep it going without Coke!
Being in the moment ~ She is Shakti with Open smiling energy.
Be more Psychedelic * you are a reflection of my heart, Feels Free.
Getting back together for this Passion ~ having to let her go in Joy.
Living Dao to the Max with a Diva.
Bill by the Orgasm not by the time

<u>The Ramayana blues</u>
Transmutation Metaphor ~ Burning Sita, testing her Purity!
"If you're Pure nothing gets lost"
Fire brings the other Elements onto a higher Plane.
The Mind transmutes you ~ through the Violet flame.
"Burn everything that is not for the Best for me and others"
Golden white and violet auras ~ Try some Cayenne pepper!
To Experience ~ waking up lighter, less dense set in gravity.
Transmutation to a Higher frequency ~ 4th to 5th dimensions.
Food for the fish ~ surrendering to the wind and birds.
"Say Goodbye in the Best way"
How you say Goodbye ~ this Understanding.
You do what you do in the moment.
You can throw it in the Ocean ~ A Conscious Process
*

<u>Samba Paradise</u>
"I am completely Open"
Having that Unity ~ "not all about getting laid"
The give and take duality dance ~ try Relativity.
Yin (:) Yang embracing together in hot romance.
Making beautiful women happy ~ heart connect.
Heightening our own Levels of total Awareness
It's just a game ~ making the Conscious visible.
We have to learn the female ~ who represents Love.
Males appreciating you * living in adoration & devotion
*

<u>Not in her Face!</u>
Shackled to each other; Pay all the Bills then we're Free for Love!
"We're here to fly ~ I'm making the music ~ here's the Acid!"
Full Power Solar shower; the Coconuts ~ You know the Story!
"One foot for me is touching the earth"
The Inspiration comes from everywhere ~
"That's all Women need is a ROCK, her Rock!"

Copulating Aliens

Psychedelic is everything * existence itself,
no Mind-boundaries to other dimensions ~
Lost in Space ~ again and again, tuning in.
"Pour your heart into the water ~"
Observing change being it ~ not in or out.
Living in the moment ~ nice and spiritual.
No time to write been dancing too much...
'The meditator becomes the meditation' ~ without choice, it's true.
"Don't just have a fuck have a full power spiritual, Love fuck"
Exchanging ~ juicy energy flowing from your hearts.
She's fucked you anyway so now let's meditate!
Chemistries in the blood ~ ultimately surrendering.
Universal butterfly ~ when Shakti's swishing around.
*

Full Freaky Nice Desires

"But she was young and beautiful and I was curious"
"How was she?" "Difficult" Sociopathic orgasms!
Fear, blockages, holding us in Earth's gravity ~
"He likes to rage, I call it Puja." Still the Flashbacks!
"The Psychiatrists pulled me in for raving in my cell"
Worshipping at the Trance church Altar at Hilltop!
"You need the MDMA capsule to dance in this heat"
Another Holy Land grab, try talking to the Cedar trees ~
*

Overlooking Fountains

"Always got a pipe in your pocket, for the moments of weakness!"
"Opium brings out ~ the Light" * Beauty in a Persian Rose garden.
Fully smiling, gazing at Domes and Minarets from a Mosaic Verandah.
What if they stopped white weddings in Tehran, banning bridal veils?
All kinds of colourful Orbs at Isfahan, feeling ~ contact with Life*Space.
They dance the Mask ~ Sufis whirling into voids of timelessness ...
An addict in the music room * In Love with Love

Shakti Hard Core
Psychedelic custard, mescaline chocolate.
Ain't got a woman, a grill, a microwave,
ain't got an oven to make apple crumble.
Spirit needs body ~ Matter to manifest itself.
"I want my smack bag back!" Fully dodgy!
Bag and Bone man sat in a crack house!
Proper nymphomaniac, loved it couldn't get enough!

*

Juicy Luce Speakers
Enjoy the music, happy, happy, happy.
"then you've made it into Goa"
'Time passing, rings of a tree' ~ forest metaphor.
"I was dreaming of this when I had dengue fever"
'Avatar' ~ they all clicked into a sacred woodland glade!
The bush's pulsing, vibrating, throbbing red ruby buds.

*

Dripping, Kundalini Rising
'Surprise Sex Law' ~ What is this kid doing with this old man,
with his tongue down her throat? You have to wear a condom!
She has to say, "Yes" or it's Rape! Caution entering a Church!
Designer Vagina catalogue, who wants to try a cliterdectomy?
Cutting your heart out, they can have the blood! Throw it in!
"The joy of letting go of All of that keeping you down!" FGM!
There are so many people who want to Suffer. How's yours?
"I don't fancy being a meal for vultures." "But you're dead!!!"
Arranged a Tibetan Funeral ~ giving it all to the Organ Bank!
Phantom of a Mind telling you what to do ~ Allowing Krishna to
manifest through you ~ without ego there would be no Creation.
You want it to be flowing ~ Ego gets you through the Mind, use it or
lose it, helps you cross the Universe. As long as there is 'I' there is
Identity with Ego ~ You want to transcend it. Don't have to lose Ego,
you make it Self-Conscious, become Supreme, merging in the divine

<u>Without Aggression!</u>
A Happy smack ~ "I think it's the powder." Her strong story!
"My ex-girlfriend snorted me out of house and home!"
"I didn't know if I was dreaming through my arse"
'Freedom is a concept of supply and demand'
"Happiness is Free from desire"
'bring the drops ~
*

<u>Experimental Man</u>
Psychedelic dal, totty and chips! Zonked out on Prozac ~
What's behind the facade of St. Peter's, lost in the catacombs?
The biggest Vatican vault of Secret Knowledge of the World ~
'That God doesn't exist' *(Except in your heart as truly human)*
Look for the solution in your-self not outside ~ loosen it up.
Don't get hooked by tragedies, temptations, all of the dualities.
Allow yourself to get that feeling by being here ~ in the present.
Reflecting their Categorization ~ letting them into their own Trust,
*then they Open up, next step is different, changing ~ r*evolution.*
Understand discernment look into the mirror inside of your Universe.
*

<u>'Chicknshow'</u>
No Olgas, no Christinas, no Natashas, all beauties gone!
"Just what happened between us? Very Magical ~
"I'm a free spirit" ~ allthebabydollscreampie.com
"I have to look after the dog" ~ "It's not your dog!"
Talking to a non-judge-mental hippie wearing a thong.
"Who you gonna please with that?" ~ "Me, of course!"
Paradise ~ must end, otherwise can't have anything new.
Nectar ~ putting things into Psychedelic Space.
Desire to fit in ~ to be themselves....
Women are going back for a bashing!
"Want to be correct with other people"
be Open

Astral Magic Island

Anunnaki, the Sumerians, Nephilim, Pharoah's,
Swiss Nazi's Octogon, Digital Virtual Fortresses.
'Capitalism' a beautiful Illusion; No Missing Links!
Go to Palenque, take some magic mushrooms.
"You'll see where the Mayans went!" Ask Chacmal.
They're still there we just can't see them; 'Donde?'
Global insanity ~ Unfolding. Ask Niburu for help.
Time to make a decision ~ make Reconnection.
'They wouldn't do that in Bahrain!'
"Yoga is Union ~ Tantra is Connection"
Life is the teacher * be OPEN.
Quality of Meditation.
*

Free All Around

Don't Ask! ~ Absence of Thought
Just Plug In * to the energy field.
Science high jacked by Finance!
Applying Consciousness ~ to manifest it.
Go into Zero frequency ~ it works by itself.
Hold onto to your Trust and let go completely into Space ~
without the idea ~ Well what about floating a Dysonsphere?
*

Viva Los Quimicos * Interpretation

Allowing ourselves to merge ~ try Raw food!
"Science is only what is allowed to be Science"
'Used Chocolate beans instead of Money' or a Tulip!
She took Guarana with her on holiday & Milk thistle.
Apply some Oxidation drops to your brain root ~
for an Implosion! 'Viva the Spiritual Proactivist!'
The 'Heart Dance' ~ "I like No Dimensions"
"You can use it, you can lose it too!"
"We are it"

Platonic Combination

Sun in your Heart * Again ~ be a wild thing!
"I'm on an Endless (Summer) holiday Baba"
Neurotransmitters Alive, took a job trimmin' weed.
California dreamin' ~ tellin' amazin' Shiva stories.
Cosmic Circus ~ "One freak knows another freak."
Going deep into it ~ using the best MMS. Oxygenator.
What the Planet needs Baba, top of 'Superdrug' Scale.
Never roast the seed it's got human energy ~
transfused in the heart with Superieur intention.
The Gods' Chocolate! Taste a little buzz…
"What do you do with your Cocoa butter?"

*

Quiet Tibet

A Genocide here, a genocide there, a genocide everywhere!!!
Then where are you, you got Vérité Sniffer and still not Happy!
Fall Out ~ drugs not a problem help me get an easier Divorce!
Gotta get the right context everyone's got different stories ~
Stronger the environment for Play the better, she'll come to me.
Dynamite in the Kettle! It's always in the dosage ~ the Healing.
It's All Balance ~ Multiple dynamic equilibrium, adjustment and
Regulation mechanisms make homeostasis possible.
The body heals itself & it's for the best.

*

Energetic Response

"It's Off the Scales!"
"I love Shockin' people"
"Isn't She L o v e l y" ~ (even to a blind guy stereotype!)
"Walkin' up and down the beach with me Freezer Box"
Vodka and Rice Krispies for Petit dejeuner. MDMA gelati.
"Add another ¼ to the Punch" ~ then my tent flew away!
Line of Perspective in a Space where there is no Space!
"Realised not thinking ~ It's the living being that I am"

<u>Mycology Chockies</u>
Find some magical technique ~ we all want to fall in Love.
All I gotta do is hold them in my hands.
The ecstasy of Magic Mushrooms ~ within.
Food of the Gods, existence at your finger tips.

*

<u>Full Moon Recharge</u>
Hangin' out with experimental, biting lesbians, spaced whirlers ~
Pukkha friends and a Sufi poet making Puja, high on pure Opium.
"More problems to deal with in India than a Sadhu smoking weed!
Stop closing parties at 10pm destroying the Energy on its rise!
Giving them the juice ~ Quality of the Gift.
Regenerating My-Self ~ Full Cosmic boost!
"I Believe in the Power of Psychedelia"
Relax have a chai, everyone was tripping and more.
Being in a great environment, freely in the air ~
Strong Ocean tides washing in and out from Venus ~
Ascending at Shiva Valley * beach, Psy*trance Party.

*

<u>Psychonautic Red Flag</u>
"I don't like Zombie films that worry me, prefer to laugh.
Danger Stoned! Spanking it in Goa; "I don't give a fuck!"
She fell for a beautiful maniac with flashes of brilliance!
Alpha women going for it! One Love ~ Babe magnets.
'Angels sitting on a bench ~ feeding the birds'
Feeling such heaven, bliss, breathing so deep
with two pairs of really famous Jailbird twins ~
Games of dualities ~ Ultimately Cosmically whole in a black hole.
A Clear Channel ~ on the edge of Knowingness, nothingness.
'Awareness that they Have It ~ they don't have to Achieve it!'
Making her Full Magic on the Stage * bit more Psychedelicate.
"You are Smashed Potato!"
'Living It ~ Is It'

White Frames of Morea
"Soyez amoureuse vous serez heureuse"
Catholic burkas destined for the unspoilt Isles of Rapture ~
Is this Paradise? Ruined by missionaries not so very long ago.
Polynesian King's buried in the uniform of a French Admiral.
'La Orana Maria' ~ "Where is Eve?" Inspirational feminine.
Took a young girl as his muse from a nearby village ~
"Will you live in my hut?" She brought her pet monkey.
Listening to Buddhist messages and Passion plays in progress!
His later pictures were the prettiest.
The beauty of a barefoot woman ~
with a fragrant flower in her hair.

*

'Le Sourire'
'Oviri'- 'The Savage' ~ wanted this Sculpture on his grave.
Packed a bag with morphine and some Arsenic ~ whilst
campaigning against corrupt and criminal Colonists.
Who's preaching Sedition?
Obvious cracks in his sanity, courage in his pain!
Caution, "Never go to the Catholic Mission!"
'Less Civilisation, more Meaning' Male & Female as One.
'D'ou venons nous, Que sommes nous, Ou allons nous?'
Carving Coconuts ~ beside the giant Tikis of Hiva Oa.

*

Cocaine Confidence
Feeling King of the World on Coke.
It's All lies!!! LSD is the Truth drug.
That's rough - no teeth at 14
No she was 16, 2 ugly sisters!
A full moon beauty dripping in the night.
"When you love it you want to lick it all the time ~"
Giving ourselves the Pleasure ~ of falling in.
"It has to come out of Thankfulness, Not Force"

Telepathic Music
What about the healing?
You are what you feel Connected with.
The Healing is the Integration.
It's all in the moment ~ Unfolds ~ breathing and falling in.
High DNA revival ~ trillions of neutrinos dancing inside you?
More possibilities of experience ~ going through the Matter.
A little circle over the Heart, out of your Personality,
letting your Masks take the centre stage and perform.
Imprint in your lines & helixes ~ you can change how it Forms.
Infinitesimal Illusions crossing the boundaries of time & space.
No more Conflicts ~ from the duality ~ if you go in the heart.
You Are The Oneness

*

Nadi * Point
'Full Temple Massage'
Doorways to the Energy ~ lakes, rivers, unblocking dry zones.
Like an old Elephant, saw a lot more of deep Character in it.
Sensitive from his trunk to his feet; saw much Bhagwan around.
"You don't need a reason ~ unless you give it a reason"
Evolution of Consciousness, of nature, of wo/man, of the Cosmos.
A living being ~ know how to see ~ taking in the moment.

*

Sodom & Gomorrah
The Illusion breaks apart, quite strong seeing that on a Trip!
What is now ~ trying to be? Calmness in any Paranoid state.
"Can't stay here, everyone sees you are not normal!"
"You fall into a boys/girls eyes and you're fucked!"
You have to throw it out ~ to Manifest it Clearly.
"Be happy you're FREE not with Love suckers on your breast"
"I do everything for you, you do everything for me!"
To be in then go out of it ~ Sit, relax, give it direction
Let it Unfold ~ Watering the Sun flowers

Concresence

I'm resonating in my silicon chip ship.
Vision of Psychedelic Flower Power ~
"Fly me to the Celestial Moon"
Interactive love ~ encountering culture.
Seeing Jewel Earth from Outer Space.
Planetary Vibe * new Astral perspective.
"Would you like to dance Magically?"
Brainwaves beating at a multi-cellular rave,
taking a Conscious trip along a Cosmic wave.
Realisation of extra sensory deprivation states.
Transcending the Torturous chamber.

*

Complete Confidence ~ with Life, with yourself ~ A beauty!
"History is shite ~ Past is Past & the Future is non-existent"
I AM WHO I AM * not a memory or Imagination; here now.
"I am being Myself " feeling at home ~ Free to Dance
Captain Potential at the Theatre of Inter-faces ~
Intuition swimming in sub-conscious Theta waves.
'When you were old enough to take psychedelics'
Spontaneous touching of superb, natural mysticism ~
Awakening to the truth of a microdot on her cherry lips.
Supersonic catalyst peaking with a human humming bird.

*

Primal energetic lights

Sublimely ~ the Heart of Unconditional Love.
Master of Illusion * travellin' inspiration,
the Outer limits ~ Nano Transmutation.
Nectar flooding through the Blue Lotus delta
~ streaming Psychedelic visualization...
throbbing in a steaming pudenda paradise,
hips, lips, legs, hair, eyes and big smiles.
Starry attraction connection

Star Rock

Cock Trek ~ better still she called me XXXXPan.
"I'm goin' back to mow the lawn!" in Maracaibo.
"You might win the rat race but you're still a rat"
Better still try the Goa Complimentary Lifestyle.

*

Sat gazing at the Klingons mate

Too much cocaine! Recreational drugs in Bishek.
"That's why I travel, I see so many beautiful things"
"I think those drugs Really dissolved the Mind-sets"
Capt Methry regenerating on the hologram deck....
being in time ~ in that space, being in tune...

*

The Exterminator

Junkie introduction ~ "You've got nice veins"
DMT; spiked in Varanasi! Couldn't stop the tears ~
Mind blown by Shiva; Dolphins spinning in the Ganges!
It can happen, it does, it did happen! Expect the Unexpected.
False, pseudo Interpretations! He thinks he can blow her Mind.
You are Free to go; decloaking her vessel; design in Organite.
Just live for now ~ unattached, living in that Perfect moment.
Atomic multi*dimensionality ~ Auric fields feeling everything.
When I met her I was flyin' high on MDMA and so was she!
Sat in a Peyote tea ceremony with Shamanic native Indians.
Made a Pilgrimage to Easter Island for the Solar Eclipse ~
A girl from Newcastle full of freckles met her at Lake Attilan.
I'm in Peacock heaven ~ with a Photon belt going off…
I'm just havin' Fun, what else is there?
Maybe she's just up for Fun too.
"Absolutely not interested in any Crazy, sexy witch"
Life is Dangerous ~ if it's not a synchronous wave
You can't be too tough, keep some in Reserve ~
Condemned to bliss ~ your Kiss

Alienated * Life Blood

Faith in Money - Monetary System Policy over the Resource.
Institutional Creation of prefabricated, massive, phony Debt!
Hallelujah! Who wants this? Ask any Financial expert advisor.
Ask those Barons working at BIS. Central Bank ~ PRIVE! IMF;
World Bank putting Conditions on who can get a cup of water!
Who has a total Monopoly, VETO, on whether you Live or die?
They are not in it to be Ethical, no human program but to Expand
PROFITS & EXPLOITATION
*

New Cloud Creation ~ Algorithmic * Alphabet

There's a 'Smart I' Transhuman being Processed.
Who is Living in the infinite Energy field?
Reflecting Understanding ~ Here * Now.
Know your Enemy ~ Know your Friends,
what is Emerging in their Amazing Conscious.
Awareness of Reality beyond the Mind's limits.
*

Forged from a Star

"You should never split an atom!"
They're meant to be ~ Cosmic molecules.
"And in come these two enlightened beings!"
Are you frightened to Open your door?
Selfish Ignorant Yobs on every wasteland, corner.
Can't walk down the street; You wanna be mugged?
'Dick head wha' yu lookin 'at yu big twat?' She said!
Wanna feel like you belong to somethin'....
like join the Army mate! Yu kno whar I mean?
You're angry and irritated with your Self Inside!
"I don't see the deceitful rat race, it ain't my World"
'Crime dived when the women could have safe Abortions ~'
Freak Economics stopping the wave of Catholic little Tyrants.
A beautiful pear tree growing in a wildflower meadow.

Liberty Caps
Full on Primary jungle ~
Surrounded by monkeys ~ rustling around.
No Pink Rooms in Iran, put some Stripes into it!
Keep feelin' each ones' ~ original vibes.
The plants told them where to find ~
the birds of Paradise
*

Still Involving
You can always get more Serotonin.
"I refused to take anti-depressants
I was happier with my Marijuana"
"The more beautiful they are ~
the more fucked up you are!"
Don't get dumped!
*

A World Classic
I'm a human not a dog, not slave karma!
Characteristics, mad as a brush anyway.
More you get right the more our membranes ~ coming together.
'Younger and Taller' ~ Rising from the cave of crystals, Naica.
In the Hall of Fame ~ Beautiful aren't they?
Have we moved into a different language here?
Nicking cobbled streets in Liverpool, they torched his car.
"Shiva me timbers ~ get on your own rollercoaster mate!"
*

Higher beings
More developed Consciousness ~
There's always been enlightened Sufis whirling in caves.
Downloaded the Coconuts, Downloaded the Crystals!
Need to create a Medicinal herb garden & organic seed bank!
You don't want to be 'out of it' ~ want to be 'in it'.
It's a Spaceship called 'Virtual Clarity Ball'

Ka* a* ba Trance
Meteorites falling from the dawn sky
Cosmic rays from stars ~ "Salute!"
Filling your garden with natural light.
Sitting on a right load of Tosh.
"Forgive me for giving...."
Fuck you!
*

Growing Tiger Farms
'Fair Trade!' ~ $600 for a kilo of bones!
A Mine of material ~ like processing dogs,
'a nod and a beep beep' ~ always learning.
"Not so innocent but very young!"
"Want a lover with a slow hand and an easy touch,
doesn't come and go in a heated rush"
"I'm unique ~ the same as everyone is"
"The Mind can't go into the Formless.
Let it be ~ silent & still, in infinite, sacred Space
This Repetitive Mind will take away the magic.
Let it be ~
*

Save the Bufo Frog
Spiritual trance experiencing inner beauty ~
'Vaastu' ~ energy panting at a Lingham hot Spot!
'It's pretty hot for an Ice Age!' My colour is the Sunshine.
Aphrodite's splashing in Primordial foam, in your garden!
Four billion year old Meteorites arriving from the Asteroid Belt
between Jupiter & Mars; 'We Are All Coming From The Stars'
Impacting on her alluring, wet Moon. It's revolving doorways ~
She's got that hippy, natural look ~ iridescent Cosmic reflectors.
Don't have to say 'No', 'Niet', 'Nix' ~ Everyone Is simply gorgeous!
Not scratching your bollocks in frustration and lust, just havin' fun.

Ninja Wing woman
Do it from Your Heart
Full Light Protection ~
Creating your own Space.
'It will be what it will be'
"Let me tell yu 'bout my mother!"
Nexus 6667890A, developing their own emotional responses!
"I will now tell you of the full horror of what now awaits you!"
"We're forever living ~ how many grams disappear at death?
"Do you like our owl?" "Is it artificial?" "Of course it is!"
"May I ask you a personal question?"
*

Live Stock - Needs!
'Cumbria may host Nuclear Waste....'
Money comes in from All directions ~
Homecoming ~ Consciousness Revolution.
'Living in the trees ~ fantastic!'
Revelation
*"I have a lot of treason!" * "I want them to know*
I know ~
*

Entwined A Winner
He's fishing, her tongue down his throat, think he's caught her!
"I'm happy to Blossom"
Preening Peacocks in the back garden…
Pressing the grapes ~ glorious infatuated head,
her feet on your feet ~
*

Holy War
"Another one bites the dust!"
"I don't know what's up with them all
They should be glad ~
to be Alive"

Anatta's C*osmosis

Concentrating on the limited Mental FORMS ~
Unaware of Unlimited SPACE * INSIDE, beyond all Mind!
Never seeing the Cosmic energy ~ gaps in between the bits.
The Empty Universe full of infinite dancing, quantum particles ~
*Missing the important, **Inside** ~ Outside. Same*Same different.*
*FULL Energy not **Things** Separating us by thought's attachments.*
Surrendering to the FORM in the moment ~ letting the FORMS go.
Giving less attention and IDentity to the Idea, duality of ME MY MINE
which is created in your Ego. Death of Illusion, woke me up from dream.
Vigilance in the present ~ realizing your essential being, be here now.
Your experience, what's within you, nothing personal matters but flow.
The One

*
*

Nature of the Beast

Want Brands Imprinted ~ All about keeping Shareholders happy!
How many 'WOW' ~ moments do you get on the M25, rush hour?
Your Reality is appearing in different places at the same time ~
Have to make the Experience to allow into your conscious ~
Feng Shui * Allowance & being Conscious about it ~ to be it
Extravaganza ~ One of those Full on Sgt. Pepper things!
Join the Army and give up all your rights and limbs!
Planning the Nuclear Strategy, really MAD in the Matrix.
Things got joined up then it got daft ~ Gave us the T word!
Disintegration of everyone except ~ themselves!
Everyone's goin' to believe in the gory bullshit.
Everyone's goin' to believe in the bloody Bullfight.
Requisition of a ghost ~ We're all gonna be haunted.
So who are You? You're a guitarist not a Terrorist!
Switched Primary to secondary polarity.
Captured by a tribe of head shrinkers.
Enlightenment on the battlefield!
What Constitutes WAR?

Brilliant brunette, dark eyed Passions.
As soon as it's in your Consciousness ~
"Everything's illegal in America" Very Patriotic!
'The rights to Life, Liberty and pursuit of happiness'
"Who owns me?" Global NWO. Neo Colonial Slavery!
"Suck my balls!" "Ask me nicely" This is your commander
Speaking! "It's a pussy Baba not a bag of diamonds"
Where did it begin and Where the fuck does it end?
Check out ... Where's the money trail comin' from?
'50% of US soldiers in Vietnam smoked marijuana'
Manipulating our FEAR, bring back Law & Order! OK!
The Universe in the Mind ~ the Mind in the Universe.
Talking myself into going to work; We're all Avatars.
Learning how to shift holograms,
Eros dancing in the dreamtime ~
Opening the eyes of your heart.
Living off Prana particles.
*

Delicious Music
Incarnation of the sweetest virus on Earth ~
You know he Condemned the condom, for eternity!
Wanting you as a Slave to the divine ~ infallibility.
Church bells on every corner ~ 5am. & out of tune.
Misunderstanding da man with the horn!
Feel the Fire!
*

Soul Queen
"I've fucked to some great tunes Baba"
Higher and Higher ~ Female Magic Goddess.
Lost the Plot ~ the full beauteousness of nothingness.
Adorably euphoric ~ amazing way to go through time.
Sweet water and a lot of Sun ~ Heading to Paradise.
Cosmic energies dancing on Earth ~

Magic Laxman Julla
Newtonian Interpretation of the Universe.
The Abstract Clockwork maker ~
"Time is a big multi-dimensional joke"
Just a Platform Aligned to a Psychic gate ~
"The angels told me to remove the "I Know nothing"
Same difference, "we don't need a mystic ~ psychic!"
Sacred music bells, gongs, ringing bowls and chimes.
"I bathed in the Ganges"
with how many Illuminated people in that river?
Brought the lightning down with a glinting Trident!
*

*5*Divorcees.com*
"I could park my Enfield there"
"Do what you want to do"
.... "I do!"
"I do do what I want to do"
"Who you gonna satisfy with that?"
"I'm gonna satisfy me!"
*

Tortoise who lost its head
All the fish are going cock eyed and the water table's lopsided!
Easy to take it easy! Bali Mushrooms, it's All One Consciousness.
Fuel injected MDMA; Coke Fiendish, where's the Glamour in it?
As soon as you make Plans ~ there's Confusion, belongs to Life.
Getting wayward people from England fighting pagan Mongols!
A Bombs, assassin drones, water boarding not with our Daisies!
It's Play Station culture for sure; How is this allowed to happen?
Only missing the super heroine with big tits and laser gun for fun.
"We got real dudes to hunt ~ We got real ducks to shoot! Hoot"
Installing in Kid's Minds, downloading 'Desensitivity Programs'
Who wants to spend their time running a Virtual Coffee Shop?
Virtuosity ~ Energy working in; Right Bring it on!!

DYNAMIC * ART * Exhibition
'Not A Broken Mind, Not A Broken Heart, Not A Broken Spirit'
'Life is Simple ~ Sharing Loving Kindness ~ From the Heart'
Paintings: Happiness, Lands of the Mind, Butterfly Wings ~
Right Time, Right Place, Good Morning La Vie, Rayon de Soleil,
Meditation Sur Un Ciel Rose, Outside the Zoo, L'Ami de Pluton,
Open Invitation, Light to Light, Sunwave, Bhavanga, Panorama,
Le Rayon Vert, Magic, River of Desires, Universe of Your Heart,
Free Spirits, Beslan, Diamond Blue, Love Chakra, Le Voyage ~
Infinity, You Are Your Own Star, Where Is the Loving?
Sunny Jetsun's philosophy is that each one of us is a channel
of Creative potential energy in relation to our interior & exterior
environments ~ He feels when we Open our hearts we express
freely and consciously this 'Art' energy of Life, which we all share.
This force is Truth & Enlightenment ~
*

Subliminal: '(psychology) Below the threshold of consciousness,
(of sensations) so faint that the subject is not conscious of them;
(TV/Media/Advertising) Technique of flashing an advertisement on
a screen for a fraction of a second so that the image penetrates to
the viewer's sub-consciousness though it makes no impression on
his conscious mind ~ (Self) A sub-consciousness mind as a distinct
part of the individual's personality.
*

Psychedelic * Hieroglyphics
"You bring the meaning to the non-sense of speech"
Celestial Crystal Space ~ beyond Ego, the Conscious Mind,
to integration with your natural sub-conscious stream of life.
Come to Goa and give up ~ Surrender to this energetic flow.
"I'm completely Open to you"
Peace, Love Not War!

ABOUT SUNNY JETSUN

*Inspired by the sixties Sunny started traveling the world in 1970.
His spiritual journey on the hippie trail to India took him through ~
San Francisco, Los Angeles, London, Amsterdam, Paris, Vancouver,
Sidney and Kathmandu to Varanasi. His arrival on the sub-continent ~
was the beginning of writing autobiographical verses capturing his travel
experiences, encounters with remarkable people and his quest for self-
realization. Combining experimentation with drugs, sex, rock & roll, art,
meditation, Love and life in general. Sunny started to open up to a multi-
dimensional Universe. He lived the mantra, "Turn on, tune in, drop out"
realising Mind's-illusions, inspired by deeper feelings of holistic nature,
empathy*energy & Space.*

*Over four decades Sunny has written and published 28 books of poetry,
created over one hundred paintings, traveled the World and considers
his masterpiece to be his daughter. He has spent the past fifteen years
in Goa, India inspired by the freedom to experience and idealism of
human consciousness.*

Sunny Jetsun books and art are available on the web at:

*Website: www.sunnyjetsun.com
Facebook: www.facebook.com/sunnyjetsun
Amazon: www.amazon.com/author/sunnyjetsun
Smashwords: www.smashwords.com/profile/view/sunnyjetsun*